The War on Terror and Democracy

An Arab American Perspective

Neal AbuNab

Published by:
Aramedia Publishing
P.O.Box 7596
Dearborn, Michigan 48121, USA
(313) 506-4409
Email: nealabunab@todaylink.com

Printed in the United States
First Edition. 1st Printing.

International Standard Book Number (ISBN):
0 9772705 13

Library of Congress Control Number (LCCN):
2006904450

To my two angels: Dignity and Respect

Contents

5

Foreword

This book is a collection of essays and articles published primarily in the Arab American News in 2005-2006, in the metro Detroit area where the largest concentration of Arabs outside the Middle East lives. I am grateful to the publisher of the Arab American News and its editorial staff for their devotion to bringing to the American people an alternative point of view. A perspective that Americans rarely hear in the mainstream media.

It's been almost five years since the tragic attacks of 9/11 which triggered the war on terror and initiated a policy of spreading democracy in the Arab and Muslim world. The name of this book comes from this critical subject that had a profound effect on people's lives here and abroad. It has affected every one from the way we look at flying to new attitudes towards religion to the way we approach social justice.

What has this war achieved so far? How long do we expect it to continue? Will there be an end to this war? What does victory look like? All these are questions that I attempt to answer in my weekly columns and frequent commentary. The Arab American perspective is unique because it appreciates the two sides of this story and it offers an insight that is missing in the US corporate media.

Most of the talking heads that dominate this debate are either extreme right-wingers or extreme left-wingers and cool heads rarely prevail. This conflict will require the United States to change its attitude and behavior towards Arab and Muslim nations. Anyone who claims that change has to come from the other side alone is in denial. By the act of war in Afghanistan and Iraq America had already changed. But many years of strife and hundreds of thousands of lives can be spared if America adopts a consistent foreign policy that respects the aspirations of Muslim nations.

What do Muslims want? What do Americans want? What does every human being want? Freedom, respect, security and an opportunity to earn a dignified livelihood. It is no mystery that America can end this war in 100 days. It can resolve the Arab-Israeli conflict and enforce a universal code of human rights on itself and on every state on earth. But America's heart is divided and it won't apply such a code upon itself. Its internal squabbles are materializing on the world stage and foreign policy is at best inconsistent.

The War on Terror has challenged the tenets of western democracy. Democracy is a movement that reflects the deep faith, culture and heritage of a nation. Post 9/11 America was transformed into a Christian democracy with a Jewish heart. The Middle East can not have a Christian democracy because its heart will always be Muslim.

Democracy in the Arab world will produce non-secular governments such as Hamas in occupied Palestine. This was no secret prior to 9/11 as the experience was tried in the Algerian elections in 1991 and the government nullified the results which led to widespread violence for many years. All over the Arab world, if so called free and democratic elections were held today, they will yield Islamist governments allied with the Islamic Republic of Iran.

The invasion and subsequent occupation of Iraq will yield in the end the exact opposite result that America hoped for. President George Bush exhausted the now-defunct argument of Weapons of Mass Destruction (WMD's), and then began peddling the idea of a democratic haven in the midst of all these dictatorships. But the democracy in Iraq will eventually produce a regime that looks more like Iran's than America's. Iraq will become a natural ally of Iran in a conflict with America.

In the past one hundred years, the Arab world has tried every type of government. They imported the secular ideas of communism and capitalism but they were applied in extreme measures always resulting in dictatorships. Monarchies are still around and they continue to thrive as they dig their heels deeper installing feudal lords and tribal chiefs with absolute loyalty to the Monarch.

The people of the Arab and Muslim world are angry and hungry. It is a volatile combination that will keep exploding until real democracy evolves from the street level. The United States will finally realize that such Islamist movements of freedom are totally consistent with its founding principles. Till then, we are in for a long and bumpy ride.

Neal AbuNab
April 2006

My 2005 Predictions

Celebrating the coming of a new year was first observed in Babylon 4000 years ago. And ever since people have been making New Year's resolutions and going to astrologers to ask if they'd come true.

Astrology has roots in most sciences like Physics and Astronomy. But most of all it digs deep into the metaphysical mysterious world. It exploits man's fascination with the innate fear of the unknown future.

It was told that Nancy Reagan held regular counsel with the "charters of the stars". She had an astrologer pick the date of December 7, 1987, for the apocalyptic meeting between Gorbachev, the Head of the "Evil Empire" back then, and her husband, President Ronald Reagan. It just so happened on that day that the first spark of the Palestinian Intifadha went off.

I am not an Astrologer but I read deep into the political behavior of nations. I try to observe the direction of waves of human sentiment. This science crosses paths with Astrology but I won't put my money on the predictions of either.

Nonetheless, the recent Tsunami has prompted many people to dabble in prophecies and forecast doomsday and the signals that God is sending to mankind. So, I will dabble.

Hasan Al-Sharni, a famous Tunisian Astrologer predicted great political turmoil for 2005; lots of blood culminating in the assassinations of George Bush in the US, Iyad Alawi in Iraq, and Mahmoud Abbas in Palestine. He also foretold of the death of Saddam Hussein before his trial and terrorist attacks in Britain.

Predicting turmoil and blood baths in the Middle East is easy. It's a safe bet and it happens every so many years like clockwork. The stars will be making their cross over in June and into July of 2005. So, please be careful if you're traveling to the Middle East at that time. I won't be making any plans to go near there during these two months.

I read the Torah and the second book of Exodus talks about the liberty of a people from bondage. "The Lord said to Moses, "when you return to Egypt, see that you perform before Pharaoh all the wonders I have given you the power to do. But I will harden his heart so that he will

9

not let the people go." (Exodus 4:21). Then, God proceeded to inflict the famous Ten Plagues upon the Egyptians. The "Plague of Blood" and then the plagues of Frogs, Gnats, Flies, Livestock, Boils, Hail, Locusts, Darkness and ending with the mother of plagues upon the Firstborn children of Egypt.

Today, the people in bondage are the Palestinians and Pharaoh can easily be Israel's Prime Minister, Ariel Sharon. The Palestinian child in the year 2000, asked Sharon to let his people go. But this child, armed with a meek stone, was no match to the power and fury of Israel's Pharaoh. The child faced off with the great big tank, and defied with his innocent courage the symbol of might on earth. But the cowardly sniper's bullet killed him. It killed the child, Faris Odeh, in November 2000. And the curse began to plague the new People of Israel. The ten plagues of Moses began its course.

I read the Qur'an, the Bible and many other fountains of the human spirit. It's easy to conclude that God's cycles come in fours, just like the seasons of the year.

I read the history of mankind and the rise and fall of civilizations. It's easy to conclude that man's cycles come in threes; the rise, the plateau and the fall. Or birth, life and death.

Putting the two together gives us complete cycles of sevens, the same as the number of days in the week.

Armed with the above simple information, I bought a couple of Astrology books, read them thoroughly and began making my own charts. I dabbled so to speak. I related the movements of stars to the cycles of God and Man. I came up with an exact date and time for the Day of Judgment.

I plugged in the dates of the Intifadhas, the Peace Accords, the blood baths in Bethlehem, the liberation of Iraq, the volcanoes, the Hurricanes and the Tsunami. According to my charts the Day of Judgment will happen on April 4th, 2009, at Noon.

My colleague Danielle Smith asked: "is that the end of the world?" I said: "or the beginning depending on which way you look at it."

Most likely, it is the end of the current World Order established by President Bush, the father, back in 1989. A World Order of Tyranny and Violence as a political system to govern people.

A survey revealed that the most common New Year's resolution for Americans was to lose weight or to pay off debt. The Babylonians' most common New Year's resolution was to return borrowed farm equipment. Some things don't change even in 4000 years; human nature remains constant. And humans, like myself, love to dabble in the mysterious nature of the unknown.

January 15, 2005

A Palestinian who wants to Vote

I call Ramallah every so often to check up on the family home. After the passing of my father I inherited a thankless job. I asked my trusted friend, on this occasion, if our Home voted in Sunday's Elections. Since its owners don't have the right to vote.

My friend always gave me the real pulse of the Palestinian Heart. He said that business is the fiber of existence. Insecurity has scared money away. There are no jobs any where, except in Ramallah. People flock there like they're coming to America.

They voted for Abu Mazen (Mahmoud Abbas) because he's friends with George W. Bush. They will grab at any straws of hope and optimism. Though, they know Sharon all too well. They know everything rests in his tight fist.

Abdul-Jawad Saleh was the Mayor of neighboring Al-Bireh in 1964. He built our Home. The stone masons hand-crafted every stone. For years, the front yard was a make-shift quarry like a scene from the Flintstones.

But the house was finally built. We were supposed to move in on June 5th, 1967. But instead Israeli tanks rolled in. We became homeless overnight.

The house was guarded by "Abeed" (Black Palestinians from Jericho). We paid them to live in it. They had a family of eight children and the old man died. Then, my father died. His half brothers coveted the house and hovered over it like vultures.

11

They kicked the "Abeed" out. They let squatters move in. The squatters said they were Fatah. In 1994, I went back to reclaim it from Fatah, the squatters, and the half-uncles.

I gained the trust of the half-uncles by marrying into them. I paid the squatters $10,000 and reclaimed the sad house. It looked like a junkyard in a Farmington Hills subdivision.

The house told me stories of the Intifadha. People were jailed in its basement, interrogated, and some lost their souls. The bullet holes in the walls whispered tales of steel-tipped heavy Israeli boots. The bomb blasts on the outer facade spoke of resilient resistance. Mortar shells only left black rings of smoke on the invincible Palestinian stone.

I bonded with the House and the land it sat on. I renovated it. I employed needy refugees from close by Al-Amaari camp, who claimed to be Fatah leaders. I gave it all I got. But the land of Milk and Honey had sucked me dry. It turned out to be barren like a wrinkled old prune. It'd become the land of perpetual misery. A land full of stones and thorns. It just produced tears in the end regardless of the noble intentions or the effort.

Abdul-Jawad Saleh was allowed to return. He is a member of the Palestinian Parliament now. He screams and shouts about government reforms and most of his words fall on deaf ears.

Palestinians are worn out by tyranny and violence, from within and from without.

I envy the Iraqis of Dearborn. America begs them to vote. I still whisper to people I am a Palestinian. But in the eyes of the most powerful nations on this earth, I don't exist.

My father and mother were born and raised in the old city of Jerusalem. My father lost a hundred of his friends in 1947 defending the old city with Abdel-Kader Al-Hussainy. He planted Jerusalem deep in the heart of his children. There is no Palestine without Jerusalem. We were entrusted with Jerusalem by Omar Ibn-Al-Khattab and we became Al-Ansar, or the people who will make Muhammad's message victorious, till the end of time, or till we perish.

The thorny issues that will never be resolved by Sharon the Pharaoh; the Right of Return; Jerusalem; and a Palestinian border without a single Israeli soldier.

Jews all over the world enjoy an automatic citizenship to my home. While we have became the new "Abeed" of the Arab nations. Poetic justice. I ask God every day to tell me of my sins and the sins of my fathers in order to deserve this fate.

Palestinian elections united and emboldened their heart. What comes next is the big disappointment. Pharaoh (Sharon) does not believe in justice, otherwise he would've let this people go. And so there will be another disappointment and another blood bath. But my trusted friend in Ramallah is not worried. He says "it can't get any worse."

As for the rest of us, the Palestinians who roam this earth in the Twilight Zone, we will insist that as long as we breathe we exist. And as long as we continue to breathe we know we are winning. Even if no one wants to open up the door and say welcome to the dinner table.

January 22, 2005

A Reverend and a Bus Rider

So money can't buy you love. But in America, it buys respect.

A 91-year old Black woman could not pay her rent in Detroit. A church stepped in to help. Reverend Adams said: "it was a simple act of kindness...we did not want to set her out in the streets."

The old lady suffers from dementia. She probably doesn't remember why she moved to Detroit in the first place back in 1957. Back then, Detroit was the "promised land". She had lived in Montgomery, Alabama. And on December 1st, 1955, she sat on a White person's seat in a bus. Back then, Blacks were segregated from Whites and had a designated area usually at the back of the bus.

But she made a stand. She refused to leave her seat.

A 27-year old Black Reverend heard of the incident. He wanted Blacks and Whites to sit wherever they liked in the bus. He called for a boycott of the Public Transportation System.

After 381 days, he was invited to ride in a "racially integrated" bus and to sit wherever he pleased. The young Reverend's name was Martin

13

Luther King, Jr. And the woman who refused to give up her seat was Rosa Parks.

A boulevard in Detroit bears her name. It would be a disgrace, however, if she became a bum and homeless on a street named after her. Economic realities are harsh, but society can certainly afford an apartment to preserve the old lady's respect and dignity. Riverfront Associates, the owners of the apartment building where she stayed felt that way too. In October of 2004, they graciously allowed her to live rent free for the rest of her days on this earth.

King became a national figure. He advocated for non-violent passive resistance to bring about equality. Then, he talked about his dream of America; a place where Black boys and White girls can hold hands and go to school together.

But many influential people didn't like that dream. So, Bobby Kennedy, then US Attorney General, authorized J.Edgar Hoover, the FBI's Director, to wiretap King and record everything he says, in private and in public, and to follow him wherever he went.

Meanwhile, his brother, John F. Kennedy, the President, met with King. They talked about crafting a federal law that stops discrimination.

The law passed in 1964. It was called the Civil Rights Act. It made discrimination illegal. It made people of all colors, religions, and national origins equal, in the eyes of America.

It was a tide that uplifted everyone. King rose to the top and received a Nobel Peace Prize. But, J.Edgar Hoover threatened to release all the juicy tapes. Hours upon hours of Martin and his private life with all the women that he consorted with.

King came apart, became lonely and felt mentally and physically tired.

He opposed the war that began in Vietnam. He said: "Justice is indivisible. Injustice any where is a threat to justice every where."

Does this story sound familiar? The war in Iraq, Aschroft the Attorney General, opposition to foreign policy, the Patriot Act, wiretapping, and secret evidence. Does history keep repeating itself? Does it tell us that repressive measures simply don't work in the long run? Does it embolden the repressed and make them more determined?

14

Any way, our friend Mr. King and his journey on this earth were coming to an end. He went to Memphis on April 3rd, 1968, to support the striking Sanitation workers. He said: "I've been to the mountaintop...I've looked over...I've seen the Promised Land...We as a people will get to the Promised Land...My eyes have seen the glory of the coming of the Lord."

The next day, he was shot dead. Riots erupted all over the nation. The streets of Detroit became a War Zone. Businesses left and Rosa Parks stayed in the Promised Land. She can ride the bus whenever she wants and she can sit wherever she wants even in her wheelchair. I pray that she has the fare for the ride.

On Monday, January 17th, the nation shut down to celebrate Martin Luther King's birthday. In today's America, civil rights have given way to economic rights. You get no respect without hard cash.

Our friend's life was like a shooting star. It delivered its message. It brightened up the skies of the human spirit, for a moment or so. It's up to us to keep the flame alight.

January 29, 2005

Doing God's Work

We had a heavy snowfall last weekend. I waited at a Stop sign and a van rammed into me. I got out of the vehicle and a black middle aged man came out of the van. His voice was loud and said that I had stopped abruptly, and that's why he backed into me.

A fuse lit up inside and I felt my hot Mediterranean temper about to explode. But before uttering a single word I excused myself, went back into the vehicle, smoked a cigarette and came back out with serene calmness.

This time he said he was sorry and offered to fix my vehicle. I told him: "I'd like to take this opportunity to become friends and collect some Forgiveness Capital. I don't want you to fix it. I don't want anything from you. I forgive you and I hope God will forgive some of my sins against others."

15

President George W. Bush is always busy collecting Political Capital and spending it. He told us on TV in October 2000 that racial profiling was wrong. We voted for him. Then, he spent that capital on Ashcroft and Sharon.

He appointed an Arab apologist, Spencer Abraham, in his cabinet so we could not complain while he spent our capital.

In his second crowning on January 20th, he promised to spend all of his political capital fighting Tyranny across the globe. The word Terrorism totally disappeared from his long inaugural speech. Can we conclude that we exited the War on Terror and entered into the War on Tyranny? But "charity always starts at home" and in one's own heart.

The English say that "the road to hell is paved with good intentions." Bush always believed that he was destined to do God's work. But God also sends Tsunamis upon people.

Pilgrims in Mecca pelted Satan with stones in the Feast of Sacrifice, or Eid Al-Adha for Muslims, as Bush was taking the oath of office. He placed his hand on the Bible, like George Washington first did back in 1789, and said "so help me God."

But God in His book says that He helps those who help themselves. Bush always described himself as a "results-oriented" person. So, let's look at the results of the first four years. His government announced this week an all-time record budget deficit of 427 billion dollars for 2005.

American lives are threatened because of an unnecessary war. A record 37 million Americans live below the poverty line. One third of Americans have no health insurance. The Education system is riddled with MEAP scores and has no idea how to advance knowledge in society. Stem cell research and science stopped so we may appease Reverend Pat Robertson and his "moral" message. These are the tangible results of the first term.

In his mind, President Bush "fixed" the Economy and National Security. Now, he promises to turn his attention to Social Security and "fix" it by sending the money to the hungry wolves on Wall Street. The same people he had jailed a couple of years ago during the corporate scandals saga.

16

His ambitious agenda extends to the entire IRS Tax Code and he will "fix" it the same way he "fixed' our Civil Rights. Democrats are accused of being the "tax and spend" Party. Bush is teaching Republicans to be proud in becoming the "borrow and spend" Party. This way, when pain comes it will be fast and swift. When banks call in the loans and foreclose on the White House.

America is an Economy. Essentially, that's what keeps people from killing each other. They tolerate each other so they can make money off of each other. The primary job of the President is to preserve and grow the economy.

But this President was born with the silver spoon in his mouth. He appointed a Mexican immigrant, Carlos Gutierrez, as the new Commerce Secretary. Gutierrez had climbed the ladder from humble beginnings as a truck driver all the way to the CEO of Kellogg company. But commerce can not advance with a President erecting walls of separation and building barriers between nations and peoples.

Bush is following economic policies that America's Clinton advised other nations not to do, back in the roaring nineties. The Mexican Peso collapsed to one quarter of its value in 1995. The Indonesian Rupiah lost 80 percent of its value in 1997. The US dollar will have to continue its decline against the Euro in order to correct the imbalances in the economy.

This President has an amusing personality and character while he insists on doing God's work in allowing the starving Iraqis to vote. They are to vote on a slate of "good" Iraqis. Why not put a Referendum on Occupation on the ballot? And forget about the slate.

But history is not kind to occupations. Not in an election and not anywhere. The President himself does not pretend to justify it.

America today is teetering on the brink of bankruptcy on all fronts.

This President is obsessed with Iraq the same way the Roman Emperor Nero was obsessed with persecuting Christians. Nero Claudius Caesar initiated the Christian persecution after Rome was burnt. He murdered his own mother and his wife for the love of power. He committed suicide in A.D. 68. He reached the same result that all megalomaniac Emperors inevitably reach. The way Marc Antony and Cleopatra went before him, and the way Adolf Hitler followed them a couple of millennia later. They were all "results-oriented."

Life is a journey. It is a way. Moses pointed to the way. Jesus said follow the way. And Muhammad fashioned the way in his lifetime. Civilization is about the way of human oneness. The way of respecting each other as equals. Good results are a natural outcome of following the righteous way.

On this auspicious occasion, the meek on this earth offer Caesar in the White House a prayer; let go of "political capital" and get on the path of collecting "forgiveness capital."

February 5, 2005

Democracy by the barrel of a gun

Once there was a big chicken who thought she was a dog. She appeared before the chicken masses and barked. The masses clapped, cheered and then retreated to their coops. They felt sorry, more for themselves than for the chicken who dared to be dog.

One day, a fox raided the coop and ate its fill of the screaming chicken. The chicken-dog barked and tried its best to defend the coop but it had no sharp teeth.

Saddam Hussein was a schizophrenic chicken. He was not a Big Dog, as they call big men in hip-hop lingo.

Remember Jay Garner, the first US envoy to Iraq, right after the fall of Baghdad. He had prior experience in successfully re-engineering the Kurdish region of Iraq in 1992.

He had it right. His solution was based on understanding Arab customs and the way they organized themselves. He took notice of the strong family bonds that flowed seamlessly to the tribal leader, who consulted with Sheikhs and pledged his loyalty to a regional Chieftain.

Nation-building is about organizing society. It is not about the construction of roads and sewer plants. Democracy is about participation and not just conducting elections.

Remember Paul Bremer, the second US envoy to Iraq. He was famous for wearing boots with his suit and tie. The boots were a symbol of the

18

kind of democracy his bosses in the Pentagon were determined to install in Iraq.

A democracy by the barrel of a gun. A democracy shoved down the throat of people. A democracy based on fear and violence.

Iraqis believed that freedom always followed liberation. But America did not send an army of lawyers and educators to speak the language of democracy.

The Iraqis only saw American boys with big toys firing big guns that hurt a lot of little people. Iraqis only saw the ugly face of occupation, where dialogue was done by the barrel of a gun.

Let's cut to the chase. Elections in Iraq were not just a good thing. They were the most excellent thing that has happened to Iraq in a long time. We want to see elections taking place in every country in the Middle East. That is our clear objective as Arab Americans.

We want to see the feathers of Big Chicken, like Hosni Mubarak of Egypt, being plucked. We want to see other chickens roasted at the altar of the people.

We want to see the new Assembly of the Iraqi people draft a constitution that safeguards the rule of the people from aspiring despots. We want to see an Arab government that has protection from a schizophrenic army General, who may wake up one day and decide to lead four tanks to the Presidential palace and take it over. Such stories only happened in the Middle East.

The last century witnessed the emergence of all these chicken-led Banana Republics in the Middle East. The next century will witness the demise of all these false states where the Arab body will mend back into its natural oneness.

But it has to mend locally first and then regionally.

Democracy has to be built on real dialogue and participation. The 275 elected members of the new Iraqi Assembly will have to draft a constitution and make it a living document. They are to conduct general elections shaping the final form of government by December 15, 2005.

The founders of America drafted a Constitution. They had it ratified by as many assemblies of the people as practically possible, at the time. This transformed the document from ink on parchment to a living organism in the bonds and relationships between Americans.

In recent times, however, the ink on parchment had become more revered than the bonds and relationships. America is looking for its own heart in Iraq. Fallujah could well be neighboring Highland Park. The only difference is that Wayne County Sheriff has not called in the National Guards yet.

Legislative assemblies in America, such as City Councils and US Congress, do not pay attention to the spirit of the Constitution, when they draft laws. Most laws passed in America, these days, are based on domestic political squabbles rather than human fairness or a sense of justice.

They reflect the way of the jungle, and the organization of the Animal Kingdom, as a hierarchy of a predator society.

That's why I always say that charity starts at home and in one's own heart first.

But one never knows, sometimes democracy by the barrel of a gun, may well be the right medicine.

February 12, 2005

The Death of Capitalism

The heartthrob of Capitalism is the Interest Rate. It secures the interest of Capital from the unpredictable chase of the value of people's efforts.

Capital doesn't like risk or insecurity. It is always looking for fertile grounds to reap income out of mulling around and doing nothing. Capitalism today is not the same as the Free Market society called for by Adam Smith in 1776, in his book "Causes of the Wealth of Nations."

He had a scant belief in the idea of profit and free trade. His Free Market had an "invisible hand" which adjusted prices of goods up and down according to supply and demand. His society suffered a sudden heart attack and died in the stock market crash of 1929. His
20

unpredictable "invisible hand" became the force of greed, speculation and unregulated corruption. His pure economic theory did not take into account the norms of human behavior.

Karl Marx, on the other hand, said in 1867 that the wealth of nations should be in the hands of nations. This made sense to revolutionaries like Lenin, Mao TseTong and Fidel Castro. So, they created a system where Principal Capital was kept in a centralized pot in the hands of government bureaucrats. They didn't know how to manage this capital and so the system collapsed in 1990.

In 1932, two men rose to the pinnacle of power on the same promise. One was in America and he promised "a chicken in every pot" to the starving masses that suffered from the depression that followed the sudden death of the Free Market society. He became President and was elected 4 times. His name was Franklin D. Roosevelt.

The other man promised his people liberty from back-breaking debt. His country was paying most of its income to Great Britain in the form of War Reparations. His nation's inflation rate reached 4000 percent as the value of the people's effort was all eaten up by the national debt. His simple solution was to thumb his nose to Britain and just plainly stop paying on the debt. He lost the elections but the President could not ignore his popular demands and was forced to name him chancellor. His name was Adolph Hitler.

Roosevelt installed central controls to reign in the appetite of the "invisible hand" by enacting the Welfare Act. Government became compassionate as needy people could apply for assistance. Capitalism was tempered by the gentle winds of social democracy.

Hitler installed central controls to reflect the value of money in the effort and ingenuity of his people. He monetized the currency. It was the second time in mankind's history that a government dared to print money without the guarantee of a precious metal like Gold. Rare precious metals had traditionally become the reserve of a nation's capital.

The first time it was done around the year 720, by the Muslim Khalifah (Successor to Muhammad), the Umayyad Abdel Malik Bin Marwan, who stamped his coins with "La-Ilaha-Illa-Allah" or "We testify to God's Oneness".

Franklin Roosevelt did not have enough capital to make good on his promise of the Welfare Society and the "chicken in every pot." He looked into Marx's social democracy theory and observed Hitler's total disregard for other nations. He came up with a middle of the line solution; we will print money but we will borrow it from the rich and give them a Rate of Return called the Interest Rate. We will market the borrowing of this money as a "good thing" in the form of Government Savings Bonds. These bonds will be sold in the free stock market, and they will be traded like any other commodity. The paper security was guaranteed by the military strength of America and had a secure Rate of Return.

Roosevelt's theory of social democracy tempered the greedy appetite of Capitalism with charity. This charity took root in the heart of America and gave it a new lifeline to outlive Lenin's communism. But both theories that chase money as the purpose of society are ultimately destined for failure.

That's why President Bush called the Social Security system a "train-wreck coming". He addressed the Detroit Economic Club this past Tuesday and promised to go to the people to sell his social security reform ideas.

Hitler's monetizing led to central authority and the nationalization of most industries. He reached the economic promise of social democracy, but by then he had cancelled out the people's vote, and became Fuhrer, the ultimate dictator. His system was a closed economic one which depended on territorial expansion and occupation of other people's efforts, in order to uphold the value of the printed currency. So, he continued down that natural path which led to the bullet in his head.

Roosevelt printed more money and sold more bonds to the rich in order to finance the war against Germany and Japan. The rich doubled their rate of return by expanding factory orders and receiving interest payments from bonds.

By the year 2018, for every person receiving retirement benefits there will be just two persons in the workforce feeding money into that system. When it started, the ratio was 16 to 1. The system will not work any more because the hungry ones receiving charity will be raiding the Principal Capital and eating it. Then, America's system of benevolent Capitalism will come to its natural end (which may not be such a bad thing).

That's the imminent danger that Bush sees in the Social Security system. But wars and occupation of other people's efforts is still on the table as an alternative to upholding the value of the dollar, while we monetize like Hitler did.

February 19, 2005

United States of Arabia

The first time I passed through Dearborn was during Christmas of 1979. I stopped at the South end, took a picture of a small mosque and loved the Arabian Village sign. It was like a little village carved up from the stony mountains of Yemen. I had never been to Yemen till that day.

The second time I passed through Dearborn was during Christmas of 1987. I stopped in at the three or four bakeries on Warren Avenue and had a homemade Molokhia at the cozy Cedarland Restaurant. I fell in love with it. It reminded me of my childhood and the streets of Beirut which I roamed while growing up.

The third time I came to Dearborn was during Christmas of 1992. This time I decided to stay. I watched the streets of Baghdad and mostly from neighborhoods like Al-Kadhimiyya take shape around the newly formed Karbalaa Islamic Center straddling Dearborn and Detroit. I had never been to Iraq till I came to Dearborn.

I love Dearborn because I found in it the Arab world that I was denied as a child. I love Dearborn because it is an experiment of how the Middle East would look like when democracy takes root in it.

The different groups that make up the mosaic of Arabs and Muslims co-exist peacefully with each other. They practice their diverse faith and they help the less fortunate in their community.

Arabs have found respect for their humanity in Dearborn. It is a colorful picture of a United States of Arabia, a second USA. It is a model when Arab states, one day, will erase their artificially-drawn borders and let that body mend into its natural oneness.

The other day, Monday 14, famous as Valentine's day, I watched my romance come to life at the Dearborn Board of Education meeting.

23

More than 50 Arab Americans spoke at the meeting and asked the board to fire a teacher who had insulted the Qur'an in one of his classes. They showed the board that the spirit of the soaring American eagle had awakened in their Muslim veins. The board was spiritually defeated.

The compelling arguments advanced by different community members did not leave a stone unturned. The teacher in question will have to be offered as a token sacrifice at the altar of the people. If not, the demands will grow larger and then the board will have to sacrifice some of its own members to satisfy the thirst of the people.

But my romantic idea of a United States of Arabia comprising 24 countries and some 350 million people is still a far off mirage. The Middle East has a political system comprised of fiefdoms, kingdoms and Banana Republics. The system has a behavior as entrenched as the most powerful systems like Capitalism and Socialism.

The system rules its own people with an iron fist in the name of national security. Israel serves a primary function of being the enemy justifying the militant behavior of regimes. The system refuses to look at itself in the mirror and say that sometimes the greater enemy lies within. It lies within the way we treat each other and the way we organize our relationships with each other.

Lebanese leader, Rafik Al-Hariri, was assassinated this past Monday and all the big powers were quick to point fingers and place blame. The biggest loser in this sad episode is Lebanon and the biggest beneficiary is the enemy of Lebanon. Secretary of State Condy Rice was quick to point the fingers towards Syria and to call for an International Investigation.

Imagine the reaction in America if Arabs had called for an International Investigation right after the tragic events of 9/11. Internationalizing the Hariri tragedy serves the primary interests of the enemies of Lebanon and may well lead to civil war again. A transparent investigation commissioned by the Lebanese Parliament is the proper course of action to safeguard Lebanon's democracy and allow its people to steer through this crisis.

The people of Lebanon must stay united throughout this crisis and hope must stay alive that other Arab regimes will gradually surrender their powers to the people.

That hope was very much alive in the late nineties when King Hussein died. Then, Hafez Al-Asad of Syria followed him in June 2000, and a few others bit the dust too. But the Superglue that held their asses to the seats of power was somehow passed on to their children.

Then came the disaster of 9/11 and Bush Corporation decided to wage a shortsighted global War on Terror. A war that extended the expiration date of most of the regimes in the Middle East. Now that the War on Terror has become the War on Tyranny, Bush Corporation has declared an open hunting season for Arab regimes.

Of course if Arab regimes fall it is also the fall of Israel as an enemy nation. But the Rice-Sharon axis wants one without the other. Iron curtains and freedom don't mix too well.

Bush loves the way Mahmoud Abbas in the name of Palestinians is going about it. Abbas is headed down a path where he will give everything up before he even gets Gaza. And once he gets what Israel views as its greatest security liability; the Gaza strip, which it gladly wanted to get rid of unilaterally, Abbas will be required to sign away the rights of all Palestinians who live outside of the occupied territories. The very thing that ethnic cleansing could not achieve.

I am a Palestinian. I did not vote for Mahmoud Abbas, not by choice but because I still don't exist in the eyes of Israel. Abbas doesn't speak in my name. Israel must ask for God's forgiveness first and then my forgiveness before it pulls out of any Palestinian land. Then, real peace can be easy because I am ready to forgive if only Israel would ask for it.

The war on Tyranny and Violence must be conducted with one standard applied across the board. The Tyranny and Violence perpetrated by the Israeli regime must be included in America's hunt for peace in the Middle East.

And the hunt has rules. Cowardly acts of violence should not be tolerated by any people as a legitimate tool of dialogue. The hunt has to be a tidal wave by the people. A tsunami of people flowing into the streets of every Arab capital to reclaim it.

That's when the dream of a United States of Arabia will become possible again.

BinLaden and the Arab Dream
Part One: America's Favorite Jihadist

I believe in the heart and soul of America. All too often, I find myself having to defend the good heart of America to fellow Detroiters. I believe the goodness in America is at the cutting edge of hope for humanity. America is a place that shows the world that one day humanity can be one family. It is possible. It is within reach.

America brings the nations of the world together and tells them that peaceful coexistence is not an option. It is not a matter of choice; it is the only way of life. And there is no other way but peace.

However, many people don't understand how I can love America so deeply and yet disagree so vehemently with some of its foreign policy. With all its media pizzaz and Hollywood glitz and glamour I believe the heart of America is still somewhat introverted.

So, when America travels across the oceans it becomes indignant, defensive and somewhat aggressive. Others only see America in the form of cabinet members or through the un-inspiring words of its President George Bush.

But they are not the heart and soul of America. They are only politicians who ride the tides of the worst waves of the human spirit. They surf on the waves of fear, paranoia, and arrogance.

America's foreign policy reflects its reckless youth as it chooses friends and foes not based on its heart but more like an eager and anxious Baby Huey who needs its quick fix and sugar candy.

Once upon a time there was a big evil empire called the Soviet Union and America was obsessed with beating it and defeating it.

The evil empire invaded a stony barren land called Afghanistan. A young Saudi engineer by the name of Osama BinLaden believed in America's promise of freedom. He was born on July 30, 1957, and came from the second wealthiest family in Saudia after the royals. He had gone to Beirut in his youth and spent some unholy time in the gardens of delight during the heyday of the "Paris of the Middle East."

26

Then, he went back home and felt guilty-stricken. He turned to Allah for forgiveness and guidance. He found his calling to do Jihad in Afghanistan where Satan ruled.

He took up arms and went to the stony mountains in late 1979. The Reagan administration found an unlikely friend and forged an unholy alliance with Osama in 1985. The CIA funneled billions of dollars through Pakistan to Osama BinLaden and his base or "Qaeda" of Mujahideen in Afghanistan.

The evil empire could not crush the spirit of the Jihadist and decided that the cost of occupation was too high. It pulled out and Osama came home on a white horse as the Chief Jihadist of Islam. (By the way Jihadist is the term used in American media and the correct term is Mujahid).

He came home in 1989 and preached freedom and dignity through going back to Islam. He was a hero followed by thousands and heard by millions. His popularity threatened the Saudi regime. They considered beheading him and be done with him. But Bush Senior does not forget the friends of America who helped bring down the evil empire.

So, Osama was thrown out of Saudia across the red sea to Sudan in 1991. He set up a network of businesses and employed thousands of starving Sudanese. He proved to be a qualified statesman as the Sudanese regime could not compete with the economic spirit of the Chief Jihadist.

In April 1994, the Saudi regime revoked Osama's citizenship and his rage turned into a volcano. He openly called for the destruction of the Saudi regime that mutilated the body of Arabia and relied on the heavy boots of American soldiers to fight what he believed should have been an Arab-Arab war in 1991. So, in November 1995 his jihidists bombed Al-Khobar US Marines complex in Riyadh. It was only the first warning shot.

The Saudi monarchy was fighting for its life. It looked towards Clinton but he was too busy with a bigger fish to fry; like Slobodan Milosovicz of Yugoslavia. So, it tried unsuccessfully to assassinate Osama in Sudan. He could no longer trust the weak Sudanese regime which leaked information and offered his head on a golden platter to Clinton. So, in May 1996 he flew out to Afghanistan.

His anger was now more focused on America because it was supporting the Saudi regime over the will of the people. In the dark corners of Osama's mind he equated himself with the will of the people. He had delivered a long awaited victory to the Arabs. They have not had such a clear victory over a major world power in hundreds of years. He was the chosen one. He was to liberate Muslims and bring back the glorious days of Islam.

In Afghanistan, the wheeling and dealing Arab found a one-eyed friend who headed a tribe and a religious army called Taliban. They joined forces and Osama put up his personal money to buy out one tribal leader after the other. A technique he learned from his friends at the CIA as he relied on his business acumen in getting the most value for his money.

Within a few short months he marched into Kabul and let his one-eyed mullah friend, Omar, declare a "muslim sharia" government over Afghanistan. The government outlawed music, blasted statues thousands of years old, and concerned itself primarily with covering women from head to toe. All men had to grow beards and follow the Sunna or the way of olden days.

Then, he turned his attention back to America. In August 1996, he made his famous Declaration of Jihad against America. Osama believed that America had become the new evil empire, the custodian of Satan, and chief oppressor of muslims.

March 5, 2005

BinLaden and the Arab Dream
Part Two: Wanted Dead or Alive

Osama BinLaden's perception of freedom was the ability to practice his religion freely. In his mind, he was a freedom fighter, a Mujahid.

Freedom in the West means pluralism, democracy, the ballot box, and the ability to practice one's own faith without fear or coercion.

The two Freedoms clashed and Islam was caught in the middle.

The bomb attacks that followed were no mickey mouse firecrackers. Up until 1996, the world had witnessed attacks against civilians by

28

gangs like the Red Brigades in Italy, the Red Army in Japan or Hamas in Israel. The scale had always been limited to a building, a café' or a disco.

The 1996 Declaration of Jihad by BinLaden was to usher in a new era of blasts that caused destruction on a massive scale never seen before. His attacks were no longer protestations or warnings but had become political in their nature and objective. He aimed to destabilize governments, alter policies and bring down regimes.

Another Arab Mujahid at the turn of the 20th century believed in Great Britain's promise of freedom. He was Shareef Hussein Bin Ali, the Hashemite custodian of Mecca whose blood directly descended from the prophet Muhammad's. He believed in the English Lieutenant, whose name became famous as "Lawrence of Arabia." He marched with his ragtag bedouin army against the ailing Muslim Ottoman Turk and liberated Damascus in 1918.

British General Allenby told him that he would become the King of Arabia and his children would rule the provinces. But the Sykes-Picot (1916) secret accord had already carved up the body of Arabia with artificial straight lines slicing the cake between Britain and France.

The British took Palestine, Iraq, Egypt and Sudan. While the French ruled over Syria, Lebanon, Tunis and Algeria. The Americans who were left out of Sykes-Picot had to claim their stake. They did it the hard way by supporting the Wahhabi Saud tribe in overthrowing the Hashemites and establishing the Kingdom of Saudi Arabia (1925).

The old Mujahid, Shareef Hussein, turned to the British for help and they told him he had to give up Palestine because they had promised it to the Jews as a new homeland (Lord Balfour's Declaration, 1917). But the old Mujahid refused to give up Jerusalem and he was banished. He died in exile in Cyprus in 1931.

His children, Faisal and Abdallah, were under no pressure or accountability to their people. They decided to join hands with the British and they were crowned as Kings; Faisal over Iraq and Abdallah over the newly created Jordan.

Osama BinLaden wanted to be some body. He was deeply disappointed with the history of foreign colonization of his Arab nation. But he wasn't considered an articulate speaker in his native Arabia. He always spoke of going "back" to faith and glory. But there is no going back except in the backward direction towards repression and starvation.

Osama's spiritual journey promised of a dark future but faith to most muslims is an evolution into a brighter future. Muslims aspired to greater tolerance, more equality and an eventual arrival at the promised destination of one human family.

Osama's ideas found a cozy home in the ignorant breasts of mostly non-Arab speaking muslims in Pakistan and Afghanistan. With the help of a handful of Arabs (no more than 2000) he was able to rule millions. He began his serious campaign of terror.

On August 7, 1998, he set off simultaneous bomb blasts in Nairobi and DarAssalam. The scale of horror and devastation was unprecedented. Within hours, the CIA had pegged the after-blast signature which clearly pointed to Bin Laden and his Qaeda.

On August 20th, President Clinton ordered missile attacks against Afghanistan and Sudan. He aimed to take Osama out but the attacks failed. Clinton himself was too pre-occupied with a bigger fish to fry. The US Congress was making ready to impeach him in the Lewinsky affair.

The failed attack emboldened the Qaeda network. Money flowed from rich Arab princes and more intelligent recruits joined the network. It became global and united by the method of setting off massive explosions against civilians to bring down governments.

Pearl Harbor was the last time American soil was attacked. But on September 11th, 2001, the attack hit the mainland and pierced into the heart of America's symbols of economic and military power. The vast oceans were no longer a shield for America.

The attack was by far the Qaeda's greatest success. Within days, President Bush pointed his finger to BinLaden and declared him "Wanted Dead or Alive." Osama had climbed up the ladder to become Chief World Terrorist.

America declared a World War on Terror. Afghanistan took the first hit and its Taliban regime was decapitated. Then, Iraq took the second hit and Saddam's Baath regime was toppled. Osama ran off to the stony hills and crawled back into a cave. The war claimed many innocent civilian casualties.

30

BinLaden was once asked about the Arab and Muslim Americans killed on September 11th. He said they were traitors and "the spilling of their blood is blessed by Allah." Their civil rights were also declared "Wanted Dead or Alive."

Last week, Secretary of State Rice pressed Arab countries to fulfill their financial commitments to the Palestinian Authority. America did not cause the division of Arabs. It only takes advantage of that glaring opportunity because it is always presented on a golden platter.

America did not create Saudi Arabia without the great urge and desire of the Saud tribe to throw out the Hashemites. America is not a colonial force of occupation and what's happening in Iraq today aches deeply in its heart and soul.

As Osama enjoys his lazy afternoons in the cave, he must reflect like I do that he'd finally achieved his dream. He took his people back to the days of faith and glory. He even took them BACK to the stone-age.

Now, he is free to practice his Islam and drag his women by their long hair in the privacy of his cave. What a long way it is from the civilization of brotherhood of man, liberty, freedom and the glory of Islam.

So, let me not hear it from any high and mighty pulpit of Islam that you want to "lead us BACK to faith and glory." Please let me practice my Islam freely and pursue my dream.

March 12, 2005

Hizbollah Targeted

I was talking the other day with an American friend who is well versed in Middle Eastern history and politics.

She had a Freudian slip of the tongue. She said: "these people don't want democracy." I told her: "what you just said has been planted in the psyche of America to justify the occupation of Iraq." It was not her fault though. This is one of the most unchecked racist remarks peddled in American culture today.

31

Democracy is an aspiration common to all people; Black, White, Yellow and even Arab.

In 1947, Arab leaders told the Arab people who lived in Palestine (now called Palestinians) to get out of the coastal areas and to vacate cities like Haifa, Yafa and Akka, so they can crush the Zionists and wipe them out before they declared a state.

These poor Arab people packed up and left. Most of them headed to close by southern Lebanon. They slept in tents waiting to go back to a land free of Zionists. They've been waiting there ever since and they are the Palestinian refugees at the heart of the Lebanese struggle for independence.

In 1945, the French granted Lebanon independence and custom-fitted the newly created state with a racist constitution guaranteed to keep the seeds of strife sown in Lebanese soil. At the time, the demographics were tilted in favor of the Christian Maronites and so it was cast in stone that the Lebanese President shall always be a Maronite.

Muslim Sunnis came next in the population staircase and so one of them would occupy the next most powerful position of Prime Minister. Then, Muslim Shi'a came third and received the Presidency of the Lebanese Parliament. Other minorities like the Druze and the Armenians had to fend for themselves. The French founded a democracy in Lebanon with a majority rule and no minority rights.

Every minority had to wrest its way up the ladder of rule.

Prior to 1945 the Muslim Sunnis of Lebanon, Palestine and Syria were one family. They had the same last names, shared similar traditions, and always intermarried. Girls were brought from Damascus to be married to young men in Nablus. Men from Beirut went to Haifa to pick up brides.

Assassinated leader, Rafik Al-Hariri, followed in the traditions of his Sunni community. He married a Palestinian girl. In the Seventies, the Sunni population of Lebanon was quickly overtaking the Maronite's. Its close alliance with the Palestinians and the PLO did not bode well for the sectarian power structure. Together, they became the most powerful community while the Maronites and Shi'a lingered behind.

Civil war broke out in 1975 and the Lebanese fabric was torn to pieces. For 15 years each sect used the help of an outsider state to gain the upper hand. The Maronites were aided by France first and then Israel. The Sunnis called in the help of Syria only to find out that Syria had ambitions of reclaiming Lebanon as a province, the way things were prior to 1945.

The Shi'a allied themselves initially with Yasser Arafat and his Fatah faction. When Arafat and his gang wreaked havoc in the South, the Shi'a welcomed Israeli tanks in 1982 with flowers and rice. Ariel Sharon made them believe that they were getting liberated but instead they became occupied.

The Shi'a turned to their spiritual and blood lineage in Iran for help. Hizbollah was founded and Syria was made to support it in the nineties by way of its alliance with Iran. At this juncture in time, the Shi'a population was quickly gaining on the Sunnis and Maronites. It still held the position of number three in the power structure.

In the year 2000, Hizbollah defeated Israel and forced it to withdraw behind the UN drawn border lines, according to UN Resolution 425. It quickly became the number one power broker in Lebanon. Its charismatic leader, Sayyed Hassan Nas-Rallah, pushed the party's agenda to the forefront of Arab society.

From death new life springs. Just as the death of Arafat gave way to the election of a more participative Palestinian Authority, the assassination of Al-Hariri set off a chain of events that put Lebanon in the forefront of a genuine democratic movement in the Arab world.

But this movement is at a cross-road. It reminds me of the same cross-road thirty years ago just before the start of the Lebanese civil war. Lebanon was the jewel of the Middle East. Beirut was the envy of every Arab capital. Will this fabric tear again?

The US administration seized the opportunity and put Hizbollah in the cross hairs just like it did the PLO in 1975.

Nas-Rallah retreated from pan Arab issues and retrenched in a sectarian defensive position. UN Resolution 1559 calls on Syria to withdraw from Lebanon, and for all Lebanese militias (targeting primarily Hizbollah) to disarm. It also calls for the Lebanese army to take control of all borders.

There was a time when Iran supported Syria which in turn supported Hizbollah. But after the May 25, 2000 victory, things changed and

33

almost reversed in order. Hizbollah gained enormous credibility and became the spearhead of struggle against Israel. Its alliance with Palestinian Hamas made it a primary target in the War on Terror.

Now, Hizbollah holds the key to the next tide of democracy in the Middle East. But it must fight with the word of Allah as effectively as it had used the sword. Its opposition to granting Lebanese citizenship to Palestinian refugees stems from purely Shi'a sectarian interest. These Arab people have been refugees for 58 years. That's enough. They have a right in any Arab land they live in. Once they can secure their basic Arab right maybe they can work on reclaiming their Palestinian right from a position of strength.

The Maronites want the refugees to become citizens to balance the Shi'a power base in the south. The Sunnis have always been married to the Palestinians and they stand to benefit the greatest from a marriage contract.

Hizbollah needs to welcome the Palestinian refugees with open arms and not to use them as pawns, like many other worn-out Arab regimes have done in the past, in their supposed struggle with Israel.

Finally, the Palestinian refugees themselves need to be asked in a referendum whether they'd like to become Lebanese citizens. Maybe their addition to the Lebanese fabric would finally bring down the sectarian constitution and any Lebanese citizen can become President.

March 19, 2005

The Path to Peace

Oneness of existence is the purpose of humanity. We are one world, one community and one human family. We all worship one God and in our hearts we accept that other human beings are equal to us and behave just like we do. Every human being needs peace, security and freedom. Peace of mind is the heaven ultimately sought by every individual on this earth.

The measure of success of any governance system that ever walked the earth is how close it came to achieving the mission statement, stated above.

34

The Abrahamic faith tradition began approximately four thousand years ago to achieve this oneness. Its prophets, starting with Abraham and ending with Muhammad, focused the human mind on organizing equitable relationships. It made objects and property in this world a tool or an instrument for man to reach a higher plane of bonding.

But human beings were created with a literal mind that shaped abstract ideas into visual objects. Thus, they ended up chasing things and property in this world as the ultimate salvation, heaven and peace of mind.

The Abrahamic faith split into three tributaries. Its heart was confused with rituals and codes of conduct. It was unique in producing a powerful class of men called Priests, Rabbis and Imams. They were the so-called scholars who administered the faith to the "ignorant" masses, the people. They created Religion out of faith.

"Religio" is a Latin word that means organization. Organized faith enjoyed its greatest glory in Europe where it ruled for eleven centuries as the Byzantine Empire. Religion pursued the path of war as the solution to achieve oneness.

People have faith. They held on to the visions of Abraham, Moses, Jesus and Muhammad. But they lost faith in religion. It had become irrelevant and distracting in the way people organized their relationships and earned a livelihood. Personal faith, on the other hand, had grown stronger and its time has come once again to break down all artificial barriers separating the people.

"Evil thrives when good men do nothing." The time has come for the people to rise and crush the voices of extremism that hijacked their faith. The voices that say women are subservient to men. The voices that blow up innocent people in Iraq. The voices that wish to turn the Middle East into a blood bath to cause a prophecy to come true.

Extremism can not be defeated by extremism. It is defeated by the collective will of moderation. Collective moderation accumulates a positive force of peace that pushes extremism back to the fringes of society.

The Anglo-Saxon civilization started with the legend of King Arthur. He established the first nation-state with the principle that "Might is not right." Legend has it that he created the Knights of the Roundtable. In time, this body evolved into a Parliament and into the modern day people's House of Representatives.

The idea of a non-religious based nation-state blossomed and in the Sixteenth century William Shakespeare became its prophet. He formalized the English tradition and gave birth to the modern English language. The idea traveled to the new world and was cast in stone in America, in the form of the US Constitution, adopted in 1789.

The British continued setting up states that behaved like islands totally separated and isolated from each other by vast seas. They got to the Middle East in the Twentieth century and carved it up into pieces, as they projected their conclusions of humanity's purpose onto Arabs.

But America improved on the idea and embarked on a journey of unity where states can be separate but equal, under a bigger umbrella called Federalism. The American ideal defeated nationalist separatism in World War II. Reluctantly, Europe adopted the ideal and embarked on its journey to create the European Union.

In the last decade, the Internet and Satellite TV united people across the globe. Cultural borders erected by fabricated nations began tumbling down. Now, everyone sees that the path ahead is towards free trade, open borders, and the dissolution of smaller states into bigger unions.

America's democracy is far from perfect but it stumbled on the role of becoming the primary catalyst of democratic movements in the world. Its current democracy is a mask for monopolistic capitalism. But the goodness in the American people still represents the best hope for humanity to achieve oneness of existence.

The rule of the people is the promise of angels, and the idea can not be monopolized by US foreign policy. Everyone is headed towards that promise.

America finds itself at a critical cross-road today. It can go down the same path of war in the name of monopolistic capitalism, where people are occupied so America can suck out more resources and siphon them to gas pumps or into the pockets of Halliburton. Or it can take a leap of faith into following its promise of creating a truly participative society.

Charity starts at home. America must begin the real work of civil rights, reform its antiquated justice system, and break down the choking interests of huge corporations. Very few Americans own a piece of its ideal. Most Americans barely keep afloat in a vast ocean whose tides are controlled by very few invisible individuals or organizations.

The American ideal is torn by its commercial interests and its appetite for consuming resources. It is stuck in the chase after money just to keep up with its insatiable appetite. America's financial future foretells that it can no longer afford this appetite. In the "ideal" participative society, money will flow as a natural outcome of equitable relationships.

America must become a role model of democratic behavior so other nations will want to emulate it. It can not force its monopolistic capitalism onto others. It will be rejected.

America must search for its Christian heart and reclaim Jerusalem as a united capital for all members of the Abrahamic faith. That's where the real temple of a United World will be erected.

Jerusalem will finally live up to the promise planted in its soil by Abraham and his progeny. Nations of the world will no longer exist and only states with proportionate representation so that every man and woman on this earth will have a one-vote that counts. A vote cast in America will have the power to change the lives of people in Mongolia.

That's how America can live up to its God-given promise of delivering oneness of existence.

March 26, 2005

Arab League: Useless and Irrelevant

This week, the Arab League held a summit in Algiers. The reaction on the Arab street was one of low expectations. The people expected nothing to come out of it and they were not disappointed.

The Arab League is a more shameful organization than the United Nations. It markets itself as the equivalent of the United Nations of Arabs. But it has much less powers and has no control over a single soldier.

It is a consultative institution whose primary job is to convene the leaders of all Arab regimes under one roof. This week it even failed miserably in this low-expectation goal of bringing the leaders under one roof, for just one day. The League has become a "smoke screen" to package Arab regimes as legitimate governors of their respective states.

Its leader, career Egyptian diplomat, Amr Mousa, eagerly praised its success and provided the audience with some warm memories. Similar to the ones provided by the comedian Iraqi minister, Al-Sahhaf, who became famous in the west as "Baghdad Bob", just before the fall of that city two years ago. One has to admire these people's ability to spin reality a hundred and eighty degrees.

This League's summit did produce some positive results. It reminded the average Arab on the street of his deep shame. It reminded him of his clear objective: to bring down all these regimes.

The League offered peace to Israel. The offer was summarily rejected by the Sharon regime. Sharon won't have a part in extending a lifeline to these regimes. In fact, Israel's regime is an extension of these regimes and it is the primary reason that kept this order alive all these years.

Israel is trying to discredit these regimes in the eyes of the Arab people. As if the regimes need help at that. But Israel is trying hard to discredit the regimes so it gains legitimacy in the eyes of America. On the Arab street, Israel is an accomplice to the crime of political illegitimacy in the Middle East.

The Arab people are tired of the useless words from these irrelevant leaders. They are tired of the personal anger and false indignation shamefully displayed by some of the eccentric leaders. They are tired of the grave errors of judgment committed repeatedly by these leaders.

The Arab people are tired of the apologies and worn out by the excuse of fighting Israel.

It's time for all Arabs to say "give me liberty or give me death". It is time to liberate themselves from fear and become free men. It is time for the Arab man to muster his courage and to rise above the personal fear for his own life. It is time for him to trust in the collective will of the people. The time has come.

The backbone of every Arab regime is Al-Mukhabarat, or the Secret Police. Some regimes have enlisted up to one in every four people to spy on each other. A single word of criticism or objection to the regime lands one in a dark dungeon for years. It is not a small thing to muster the courage to criticize any regime.

Inevitably, the will of the people will awaken. It is God's promise.

These dictatorial regimes rely on fear as a primary tool for survival. If I am afraid and every other person is afraid then the regime stays in power. But I am worn out by the injustices committed. I am deeply ashamed of the rampant incompetence, nepotism and corruption that these regimes paint as an acceptable way of life in the Middle East.

Once there was an honorable man who took care of his ailing old father. The wife grew tired of taking care of the crippled old man. She convinced her husband to take the old man to a nursing home.

On the appointed day, our honorable man asked his son to fetch him a rug from the basement to carry his old man on it. The teenager disappeared for a while. He finally emerged from the basement with a small rug in his hand.

"What took you so long?" asked the father. The bright boy answered: "I was cutting the rug in half and saving the other half for you, daddy, when you grow old, and I have to take you to a nursing home."

Shareef Hussein Bin Ali is the Arab leader credited for sparking the Arab Revolt and creating the modern day movement for Arab liberty. He concluded in 1916 that his beloved muslim Ottoman empire was in fact on its death bed. The British told the Shareef to give up Palestine so the Jews can establish a homeland there. He refused.

His children; Faisal, Ali and Abdallah, watched their father sell the old Ottoman master in favor of a new attractive mistress, the British. When it was their turn, they had half of the rug ready to retire the old man. They helped the British banish their own father to Cyprus where he died a broken man in 1931.

The children became kings of Syria, Iraq, Hijaz and the newly formed Jordan. King Abdallah met with his Maker on the hallowed grounds of Al-Aqsa Mosque in Jerusalem, by a bullet from the people in 1951.

His brothers met with a similar fate in different parts of the Arab land.

Ever since, lesser men have learned that in order to have a successful Arab regime one must please the mistress, the British. Also, lesser men aspiring to inherit a regime must always fashion the retirement rug for their higher ups, who dared to say a small No to the mistress.

The new mistress now is the United States of America. And lesser men are falling over each other panting to please this mean mistress.

America has no respect for suck-ups and people with no dignity or respect for themselves. America is letting go of these regimes finally. However much they try to please is not going to be enough. The only pleasing that America requires of these regimes now is to step aside.

Hosni Mubarak of Egypt complied with America's new wish very peacefully. He is stepping aside and his son won't be running in the presidential elections scheduled in September 2005. We have great hopes that the mother of the Arab nation, Egypt, shall rise within the next six months and shall finally have the legitimate rule of the people.

(Writer's footnote: Egyptian President Hosni Mubarak reneged on his promise of stepping aside. In July 2005, he declared that he was seeking a fifth term as Egypt's president, and was "elected" in September 2005).

April 2, 2005

Road to Palestinian Unity

I salute Mahmoud Abbas for his outstanding performance in the first 100 days as President of the Palestinian Authority.

Last week Libyan leader Moammar Al-Kaddhafi called the Palestinian people "stupid", at the Arab League summit. Abu Mazen, Abbas's nickname, later reacted to the media by saying: "we respect everyone's opinion but we have reservations about some of the phrases used by Kaddhafi." He displayed the kind of mannerism and moral values that represent most Palestinians.

I am a Palestinian and I kindly ask Kaddhafi for an apology just to stop the use of such words, because they are endless when we begin to lob them at each other. Now, all Arabs have made mistakes and especially

40

their leaders. They were all grave errors that began in 1916 when Shareef Hussein Bin Ali decided to make the British his allies.

.

Managing complex relationships and keeping differences united under a larger umbrella has always been the Arabs' greatest challenge. In the past, each tribal leader or feudal lord has fallen into the temptation of settling differences using violence. Arafat went to war against King Hussein in Jordan in 1970. The Lebanese split into factions and duked it out for 15 years. Then, Saddam Hussein battled with Iran for 8 years. He invaded Kuwait in 1990 and brought the idea of unity through violence to an end.

The resolve of Abu Mazen to keep the Palestinians united paid off this week. Hamas and Islamic Jihad declared that they will join the umbrella of the PLO (Palestine Liberation Organization) and will take part in the legislative elections set for August.

The intense dialogue between the parties was carefully managed by Abu Mazen. He set the democratic tone, and the language of most Palestinian politicians followed the shift. They no longer talk about monopolizing power or having the luxury of making strategic decisions without consultation with other parties.

Wars are fought with words, claims and counter-claims. The United Nations Security Council, the courts and public opinion are the battle fields. The strongest military in the world can not justify its occupation of Iraq. The word reigns supreme, always.

The Palestinian cause has always been a media campaign. It is not an armed struggle and what has been taken by force will not be recovered by force. So long as Israel is bankrolled by America. Abu Mazen recognizes this fact very well and he is careful to inject the phrase "by peaceful means" in every objection he makes to Israeli policy.

The Palestinian cause is a media campaign targeting the hearts and minds of average Americans. If polled, I bet most Americans think that Palestinians have a country and that they're fighting with Israel to get a piece of its land. Public opinion in this country was molded over fifty years of one-sided journalism, and a media that is programmed to tell the story of Arabs through the eyes and views of Israelis.

Suicide attacks against Israeli civilians receive incredible publicity in America while the continued bulldozing of Palestinian homes and infrastructure is hardly noted. The daily suffering of Palestinians languishing under the yoke of occupation continues to be a subject hardly covered by the US media. Why? Because we have not made a bond with the American people like Jews have. Our primary purpose in America is to reach out to Americans and embrace them with love in order to fix the hatred caused by Bin Laden. Then, they will care for what we care about, and they will care to cover the issues dear to our heart.

Palestinians everywhere must be united no matter how different their political persuasions had gotten in the past. The umbrella of unity is their genuine intention to achieve peace.

Now, there is a thousand ways to skin a cat and Abu Mazen has proven that he will not head a puppet regime for the Sharon government. Justice and equitable relationships pave the road to unity. This must be practiced as an internal philosophy governing Palestinian-Palestinian relationships and then extended to the Israeli people.

Sharon does not believe in democracy for Arabs, and so he made a bet that elections in the occupied Palestinian territories will produce leaders weaker than Arafat. In fact, the exact opposite happened. Democracy strengthens a people's resolve and makes differences of opinion an asset.

The PLO made a decision in 1988 to recognize the existence of Israel and engage in a peaceful dialogue to resolve the conflict. Hamas, with its politically chaotic militant strategy has served the enemies of the PLO. These are the same people that don't want the Palestinians to have a state of their own. It's time to unite all military forces under one security group directed by one political leadership; a legitimately elected government of the Palestinian people.

The PLO and especially Abu Mazen can not allow Israel to dismantle the infrastructure of Hamas. It has proven itself in the areas of social work to be capable and effective. It has set up hospitals, shelters for the homeless, and cared for the orphans. It has become part of the Palestinian social fabric.

Israel claims to target Hamas but in fact aims to destroy the social infrastructure of the Palestinian people. Sharon will pull out of Gaza and then hold Egypt accountable for its administration.

As for the West Bank and Jerusalem, Israel intends to intensify its settlement activity so that the only option left for the Palestinians is to go into a confederacy with Jordan. Palestine would be a collection of cities run by locally elected mayors and councils. It will have no borders.

Sharon's plan is to dissolve the Palestinian identity into the ocean of Arabs. But Palestinians are Arabs and if they find their identity then Arabs will find that identity too.

But Abu Mazen and all Palestinians are onto that plan. His firm stance against the expansion of the Maale Adumim settlement is one of "life and death" for the Palestinian state. It is their last chance to make the case for an independent Palestine with contiguous land connecting it from Jenin to Rafah. It is their last chance to make the case for independent borders. It is their last chance to make a case for Jerusalem.

It all rests now on the desk of President George W. Bush as he ponders the most critical position his administration has to make, if it intends to deliver on its promise of a Palestinian State.

April 9, 2005

Life needs Death

Death is always hovering all around us. It swoops in once in a while and grabs one of us. We breathe a sigh of relief. It's not my turn yet.

Death is inevitable. It is part of life. We are scared of it because we want to live.

Eventually we learn to respect it. But we never make peace with it.

We want to live forever. So, we invent religions and create concepts of Gods and think we are safe. We tell each other that our souls live forever in heaven.

Our mind-soul-body is all one. It is indivisible. Once we die we are dead. Period. No one ever came back from the other side and told us about heaven. But we must believe otherwise we can not create a human civilization. And so belief is the core of organized society.

43

Pope John Paul II, the pinnacle of Christian belief, died this week. He was a good man who led the largest political organization on earth.

Death spares no one from its righteous claim. And from death new life springs, always. In April of every year Death somehow intensifies its activity. It is a cycle synchronized with nature. Last week, many famous people died in addition to the Pope's death, including lawyer Johnnie Cochran, Prince Ranier of Monaco, and Frank Purdue, to name a few.

Earlier, Terry Schiavo, whose feeding tubes were severed, gave in to the Prince of Darkness. Martin Luther King was assassinated in April 1968. The stock market crashed in April 2000 wiping out trillions and trillions of dollars.

The ghost of death works overtime in the Middle East. Every disaster in recent history has taken place in April. The Dier Yassin massacre in Palestine was in April 1948. The Qana massacre in Lebanon was in April 1996. The Jenin massacre in Palestine was in April 2002. And Baghdad fell in April 2003. It is now the end of the first week of April and I pray that Death finds a lucrative business in another region of the world this year, for a change.

We can not feel angry with Death. It is final. It is solemn and it is serene. We can fight the forces of death imposed upon us by other people, but we can not fight death itself.

Death is the rightful claim of the Will of Existence. So why are we scared of it? Because we have a moral obligation to the Will of Existence that as long as we breathe we must resist it. We must build a culture of life.

The procession of death always intertwines with the procession of life. But, hope springs eternal from the human spirit. And so we must always create opportunity for life.

Death commands forces as strong as life. It is the anti-thesis of life, and thus completes the cycle of existence. Death is in every fiber of our existence and without its benevolence we actually can not live. Old worn-out cells in our body surrender themselves to death while healthy ones surround them, feed on them, and then eject the waste. Every single cell and fiber in our body is replaced and renewed in a complete cycle every seven years.

Planets are like cells. They lose their magnetism and drift towards a black hole in the universe where they are completely disposed of. It is the cycle of existence and death works tirelessly to keep up with life. It becomes a little lazy in early July when the holiday spirit is in full swing.

Death is most active and strikes hardest at the two extremes of society. Extreme poverty and extreme richness are the most fertile grounds for death.

People in America die of excess while people in parts of Africa and India die of deprivation of food. People in America are waging a war with food because it is killing them, while people in some other areas are scouring the dry earth looking for a green leaf.

But God is the ultimate Force of Equalization. He works His magic and applies it to the extremes of society and recreates balance. He wants people to understand Death and respect it. But He doesn't want any hope to be lost by death. On the contrary, He wants us to have hope spring eternally from our spirits.

In Islam as in Judaism, a dead man is honored by burying him the day following his death. His lifeless body or face is not paraded for anyone to look at. His face is covered with a shroud so his loved ones will always remember him alive and vibrant, the way his spirit is. The spirit of a dead man lives in the breasts of other men who follow his ideas and message.

The Prophets Abraham, Moses, Jesus and Muhammad are all well and alive today. Their ideas have flourished and their spirit lives in the breasts of over two billion people on this earth.

This week, the Kurdish leader, Jalal Talbani, was elected by the Iraqi Assembly as the new President of Iraq. It is God's force of equalization doing its work in the Middle East.

It is a far cry from the Eighties when Saddam Hussein was the force of life in the Middle East. The Kurds and Jalal Talbani were running bare-footed in the rocky hills begging the world to give them a tiny state of their own. Everyone opposed them. There are 30 million Kurds spread in that region between Iraq, Turkey, Iran and Syria. They are all Sunni Muslims.

But it seems like the forces of division and death are headed on a declining curve in the Middle East, finally. God has accelerated His forces of Unity and Equalization, where the "meek shall inherit the earth."

And so the meek in Iraq who represented the forces of division are now in power and they preach the forces of unity in Iraq. Arabs need to defeat sectarianism.

The Kurdish community is an integral component of Arab society. The last time all Arabs were united was at the hands of a Kurd from Iraq; Salah Ed-deen Al-Ayoubi. Pope John Paul II visited the Umayyad Mosque in Damascus a few years ago and refused to stop at Salah Ed-deen's grave and pay respect to that great man who expelled the crusaders from Jerusalem, in 1187.

But the Pope was gracious enough to apologize to all the Jews for their persecution by the Christians.

April 16, 2005

America parts ways with Zionism

These are exciting times. They are historic for the Arab world. In a speech commemorating the second anniversary of the fall of Baghdad, President George Bush likened the event to the fall of the Iron curtain in 1989. That was the end of the Cold War. So can we begin writing the obituary of the War on Terror?

To his credit, President Bush has managed to reshape the tone of his foreign policy agenda in the past four months. He does not have another election to worry about. He seems at ease with spending political capital that America has collected over long years of unwavering support to some groups. And that capital has grown so large especially with Israel.

It is time to spend it. Bush's foreign policy in the past two years since the invasion of Iraq has concluded that Israel can no longer be the custodian of America's interests in the Middle East. It will conclude soon that Israel is part of the problem and not the solution. It is only a matter of time but the course has shifted and the future collision is inevitable.

America can not support the occupation of a people and it has made that clear in Iraq, as it struggles to rebuild the security forces that it had destroyed when Paul Bremer "debaathified" Iraq and purged it two years ago. Its policy must stay consistent throughout the entire Middle East as it needs to open up this huge market.

And so America has decided that Israel's occupation of Palestinians can not continue either. America has tied the withdrawal of its troops from Iraq with the withdrawal of Israeli troops from Palestinian land and the establishment of a Palestinian State. This, I predict, to happen by the fall of 2006.

On Monday, Bush held a joint press conference with Israeli Prime Minister, Ariel Sharon, at the ranch in Crawford, Texas. He said "the United States supports the establishment of a Palestinian State that is viable, contiguous, sovereign, and independent."

This affirms his earlier commitment made on November 12, 2004. The tone of Bush's voice had that familiar steely determination that we'd all grown to love or to hate so much. The tone of "wanted dead or alive" or "you're either with us or against us." I dreamed of the day when that tone was going to be used with Ariel Sharon. It seems like that day has come.

For the past three years we lived the wrath of that tone of voice. Bush's policies destroyed the lives of millions of Arabs around the world. Domestically, he unleashed Ashcroft on us who made our lives a living hell. In the Middle East, he let Sharon demolish Palestinian society. He sent US troops to Iraq to disarm Saddam Hussein but ended up with an agenda that is painful to us in the short term but ultimately benefits every Arab, once democracy takes root in Iraq.

I like this second term. It seems like Bush is picking up where he originally wanted to start right before the nightmarish events of September 11th. His agenda is shaping up on the side of every ordinary Arab. We want democracy so bad and we agree with Bush's overall objectives. However, we greatly disagree with the painful methods and dictatorial tactics to get to the promised land of Arab democracy.

This week I expected to declare the death of the idea of an independent Palestine, as April has traditionally been the month of death and disasters. The expansion of a key Israeli settlement in the West Bank will make the idea impossible. Maale Adumim, which I visited ten years ago, houses approximately twenty thousand Israelis and if allowed to expand it will connect with Jerusalem thereby cutting off Arab East Jerusalem from the rest of the West Bank. It will be the end of a "contiguous" state.

But Bush surprised me when he reminded Ariel Sharon and Israel of its obligations under the "roadmap for peace" to freeze all settlement activity. Sharon has dictated Israel's policy to the US for the past three years. On this issue, Sharon did what he usually does by elevating the firm position in the homeland and painting it as a "done deal". Then, he comes to America as a formality to seal the policy and have it blessed. But it did not work this time.

Bush gave it to Sharon squarely between the eyes. He told him to freeze all settlement activity in the West Bank. Of course, for those of us who know Zionism intimately, they also know that this was the bullet in the head of that racist ideology. Israel is a state founded on Zionism. Zionism is the displacement of Palestinians and the replacement of that population with European Jews. The death of Zionism means the death of the theocratic state, and the beginning of the transformation of that country into a democratic state.

This is the second time Sharon goes up against Bush and loses in the past month. Sharon had threatened to destroy Iran's nuclear installations the same way he did Iraq in 1981. But the US had agreed with France and the European Union that it will take a breather from military adventures for the time being and will try diplomacy for a change. They agreed to do negotiations with Iran and to resolve things with words.

Sharon had to eat his words last night on CNN. He said he will not attack Iran's nuclear installations.

Former Secretary of State, James Baker III, said in a senate hearing back in December 1990, right before the first Iraq war, that America must begin to "put in place security structures" in the Middle East consistent with its interests. The interests of America do not lie with Zionism. The two move in opposite directions. The US needs Iran to develop nuclear weapons. It needs Iran to act as a deterrent to Israeli hegemony. Otherwise, Israel will become bigger than America and will hold the key to America's future, not just in the Middle East, but in the world.

48

Americans are a tolerant people and they let Israel lead them in that region of the world for a long time. But there is a limit to everything. Even patience runs out and it has run out with Israel. America does not want to go to war with one billion Muslims around the globe. On the contrary, it wants peace with them.

April 23, 2005

Arab money has no Value

Once upon a time I used to be a starry-eyed believer in Arab American organizations. I was so excited that our community had so many organizations and they were all empowering our community. I was an active member of most of these organizations. In the Arabic festival of 1998 I went around signing up new members for the ADC (American Arab Anti-Discrimination Committee). I had great success with Arab Americans who were either poor or came from the middle class. But I hit a snag every time I approached a rich Arab.

I sat down at a bench with a millionaire Arab who refused to give up $35 for the yearly membership. He did not believe that organizations were the salvation of Arabs in this country. In fact, he believed the opposite was true. We had a gentlemanly argument for almost an hour. I failed to sign him up. He was adamant. He believed that organizations impeded the progress of Arab Americans into the mainstream of America. He believed that strengthening the organizations was like strengthening the illegitimate governments in the Middle East. He had a point that I ponder till today.

My point was that the collective spirit of our community needed a spark. No matter what happens to the organizations and what they do was not my primary concern. I was most concerned about effective representation in American society. I wanted Arabs to act as a collective instead of stubborn individuals, as they do all the time.

He thought his money or his $35 empowered me, since I was representing an organization. I offered to pay the $35 fee because I wanted him as part of the union more than anything else. He accused me of being a good salesman who reeled people in by putting them to shame. I had no intentions of shaming him. All I wanted was a union of Arabs with the most diverse opinions. It was the equation that eluded me all my life. How could other people believe in a union while

I've never met an Arab who truly believed in the idea of Union. And the Arabs who believed in a union usually benefited personally from advancing the idea.

I was always a volunteer. Never made a dime on advancing the idea of a union. In fact, it cost me a lot of money and a lot of headaches over the years. But I grew to respect the Arab millionaire's opinion. He knew his people well.

I see him at the mosque every once in a while. He tells me that he pays his "Zakah" (alms) regularly and it amounts to thousands of dollars a year. He tells me that this is real charity and not these organizations. I tell him: "yes, of course, Zakah pays your way to heaven, while organizations don't give you anything personally." He nods in agreement while it reminds me of the Popes during the two hundred years of Crusading history. They used to issue "deeds to heaven" to all the "believers" on their way to fight in the holy land.

It is the mark of the dark ages of any civilization when its richest members grow to believe that the way to heaven is bought with money. Many Muslims believe that their faith is individual between the person and his God. This is correct but they go on to justify to themselves that whatever they do to other men does not affect their relationship with God. That is incorrect.

They oppress other Muslims with their money and then they go to the mosque and pray for forgiveness. And God is All- forgiving. So, He forgives them and they go on about their business doing the same thing over and over again.

My millionaire acquaintance went to Hajj in the year 2000. When he came back I asked him if he would continue cheating his customers the way he always did. After all he had gone to Hajj (pilgrimage to Mecca) and absolved himself of all past sins. He'd come back with his slate wiped clean. It was a good time to start doing things the moral way so that forgiveness is not needed.

He said: "Astagh-fero-allah-al-azeem" which means "I fear the almighty God, I do no wrong." A couple of months later I heard from customers that he was back to his old tricks. A couple of years later he went to Hajj again. When he came back I asked him: "do you need to go to Hajj every two years, is it that bad?"

Of course, we hardly talk any more. I have no respect for his money or his values.

I would love to go to Hajj one day. But I can't quite digest the idea that some ritual is going to wipe my sins clean. I try to make peace with my sins through deeds with other people. And through righteous deeds with other people I seek forgiveness every day.

Saudi Prince Al-Walid Bin Talal is one of the richest men on earth. He has a lot of money invested in the City of New York. Right after September 11, 2001, he handed a check of $10 million dollars to the city's mayor, Rudy Giuliani.

The mayor sent the check back after Al-Walid asked America to examine its policies in the Middle East, which caused September 11th to happen.

Prince Al-Walid was more interested in protecting his assets in New York and separating himself from his fellow Saudis who had just destroyed the twin towers and killed three thousand people. His ploy of charity had backfired and it diminished the value of dignity of every Arab.

Mayor Giuliano was interested in riding the wave of Arab hate. He had no intentions of refusing Arab money. Quite the opposite, he coveted all of Arab wealth and knew that Republicans wanted to hold the key of value to Arab money.

Arabs come to America like most immigrants for its money. They absorb the worst of its individualistic selfish culture. Many become millionaires but lose the human value of their money along the way.

Money is a tool gifted to some people by God, so they would use it responsibly to advance forgiveness and equity. But most want to horde it and use it as a yoke to enslave others. When Salah-Eddeen Al-Ayoubi died, the last unifier of Arabs, he had seven golden Dinars in his personal account.

April 30, 2005

America's Collapse in Sight

How can America be in danger of collapsing?

Every empire that ever walked the earth had its heyday and its final day. No empire of man lasts till the end of time. The Greeks had a great civilization four thousand years ago and a dispute over a woman named Helen brought their world to an end.

The Byzantine Empire lasted a thousand years and it came crashing down upon the heads of the priests obsessed with controlling every detail of man's life. The Ottoman Empire lasted seven hundred years and in the end gave up the Arabic alphabet, and now Turkey wants to shed its Muslim character.

Nations are like individuals. Their greatest strength eventually becomes their worst nightmare. America prides itself on pluralism and the rule of law.

A pluralistic society lives by the diversity of ideas and feeds on the richness of multiple cultures. America achieved that ideal and it peaked in the year 2000, and it started rolling downhill after that. It has experienced an explosion of information. Too much of a good thing is as good as too little. People surf through hundreds of channels on their TV stations and still don't know why America is fighting a war in Iraq. They listen to so much information and absorb very little. They retain very little knowledge. They see things outside of their immediate surroundings as strange, disconnected and hostile to their daily lives. The only thing they care about is a job and paying their bills at the end of the month.

The Rule of Law has suffered tremendously. America's politicians are afraid of regular policemen. Prosecutors receive medals of honor when they dishonor politicians or put someone like Martha Stewart in jail. All the while they are penalizing society for the behavior of individuals. Republicans speak of less government while the air we breathe is soon going to be taxed. There isn't anything about man's life that has escaped the knife of regulation. Government has legislated every conceivable law and turned our lives into a legal nightmare.

The courts are clogged up and over three million people are warehoused in America's prisons. Soon, America will be a police state. The ideal of justice is lost in the zestful pursuit of "rule of law."

And the people who act as jurors behave like a mob hungry for blood and vengeance. Very few people have a chance of acquittal in front of a jury of their "peers". In fact this concept of "jury of peers" never materialized. A jury of Michael Jackson's peers would consist of black musicians. And for Arab American business owners charged with supporting terrorism, they should be judged by a jury made up of Arab American business owners.

The great education system graduates people who can not fix a toilet in their house. The country's foundation rests on the premise of economic opportunity. But people no longer seek honest work. They look for a paycheck and a place to clock in their hours while they pretend that they are producing something useful.

Inner cities are plagued with violence, gangs, guns and drugs. On top of that they are run by incompetent local governments and mostly corrupt mayors. No one wants to pay attention to these cities as if somehow they will just go away, on their own.

Government is not concerned with fixing people's lives any more. The night Martin Luther King was assassinated he wrote a sermon which was never delivered. It was titled "why America will go to hell".

America is obsessed in its chase after money. But capitalism will collapse just like communism did. Earth was never ruled by one super power that created a single will of existence. Two poles are always needed to create a culture of life. Man can not exist without woman. And America can not exist without an external enemy.

Every empire collapsed in a blink of an eye, and it started with seemingly small events.

Every nation's purpose must be underpinned by a humanly worthy ideal. It must be driven by a sense of purpose that is good for all people. America is an economy that depends on free enterprise, inventiveness and ingenuity. But big fish has been eating smaller fish and huge conglomerates are taking over the economy. The majority of the economy is being controlled by a handful of corporations. They keep merging into bigger whales thereby creating a false perception that real value is being created. Then, they crash burning up the wealth of investors and consuming people's life savings.

The bigger the company is the more it behaves like a bureaucratic giant that offers little creativity and new ideas. And Americans are becoming programmed that salvation lies in working for a giant company that offers a stable paycheck and secure benefits. They are programmed that life lies in performing repetitive robotic tasks all day long.

The economy has been the basis of every successful human governance system and not just America's. The challenge has always been and continues to be providing opportunity for people to pursue a dignified livelihood. Honest work gives a human being dignity. The economic engine of America is running on empty. It has no belief in the effort of its people any more. It depends primarily on the industry of war machinery and exploiting the oil resource. President Bush suggested this week that we turn many closed down military bases into oil refineries. They are the only two industries that he ever cared about.

I came to this country over twenty five years ago and I always believed that America was an ever gushing spring of fresh ideas that managed to renew itself, against all odds. But now, I truly believe that America is stuck. I give it four more years to get out of this rut or collapse.

On the long timeline scale, invading Iraq may appear like a small blip in America's two hundred years' plus march. But it may prove to be just like Nero's persecution of Christians. An event that eventually unthreaded the entire empire.

May 7, 2005

Arab Women Rights

The mark of a successful civilization is how much freedom it affords to its women. And how much freedom do Arab women have? Can anyone name a living Arab woman who gained fame in fighting for freedom of women? I can't name one. Are Arab women free to do what they want to do? Does freedom mean sexual liberation? Does freedom come without a cost? Is Arab woman dominated by the wishes of her family? Do Arab women dare speak out? Do Arab women really want any more freedom?

54

My good friend Don Unis always tells me that Arabs have one asset that will never run out. I guessed that it was their oil. He said no. I said their false bravado. He said no. I said their art of talking so much and saying so little. He said no. I gave up. He said the hips of the Arab woman. He is right. Those hips are a human factory.

Most Arab women are still wedded the good old fashioned way; arranged marriages or through introductions made under close family scrutiny. An Arab woman holds the key of honor to the Arab man. Most of the social problems that plague Arab society stem from the relationship of Arab society with the Arab woman. The Arab woman is bound by endless norms that she must adhere to. Her reputation is everything. Once it is ruined her chances of being part of that society are almost ruined. And her reputation lies in the way she conducts herself with males.

In the pre-Islam days and especially in Mecca where all cultures met, Arab women walked around in the markets baring their breasts. Arab men viewed women as prized possessions. Whenever a man wanted to honor a guest he offered him his "wife" to sleep with. Men had many wives and there was no limit on how many wives a man can have. His money bought him as many women slaves as he could afford.

Back then there were two types of Arab women; the slaves that formed the majority and a very small class of highly dignified women supported by powerful families. The dignified women formed the link of alliances between big tribes. Their demands were met by the husbands because they had an entire alliance of commercial interest riding on the relationship. These women rarely appeared in the marketplace. They stayed away from the sight of common men and if they ever had to go out to the street they clothed themselves from head to toe. Their clothing and their brisk manner of step gave an indication to other men that they were women of great honor backed up by powerful tribes.

Common men did not dare look or interact with the fully clothed women. There was retribution to having an accidental innocent interaction with these women. They gave a very clear signal to men that they were not approachable.

Men of great honor, like Omar Bin Al-Khattab, viewed female offsprings as either a curse or a blessing. A female baby was a curse if she brought destruction of livelihood or loss of wealth with her birth.

Thus, men like Omar took their female babies out to the desert and buried them alive.

Islam liberated women and slaves and made them equal to all men. Later on in his life when he became the Khalifah (Successor to the Prophet Muhammad), Omar recalled with tears dripping down his cheeks how he buried his baby girl in the sand. His girl loved him so much that she was cleaning the flying sand off his face as he was burying her.

Women in Islam were told to cover the parts of their anatomy that caused temptation to man. Walking with bare breasts in the streets was no longer acceptable. Then, great alliances were made by the Prophet through his thirteen marriages. Many great tribes became his relatives by marriage. In order to emulate the prophet and gain more of his favor they began tying their honor with his honor. Thus, these tribes began ordering their women to dress from head to toe and to cover themselves, and to act like the dignified class of women did, in the days prior to Islam.

And so the tradition of women covering themselves endeared and found its way into the Muslim culture. In the middle ages and about five hundred years ago women of all cultures and on all continents were covering their hair and wearing lots of clothes. Even the statue of liberty that stands as a symbol of freedom is fully clothed from head to toe.

Being fully clothed gave dignity to women and signaled to other men that they demanded to be treated with respect. Wearing a Hijab (head cover) is more of a cultural thing than something ordained by the Qur'an. It has become a highly contested symbol in recent years where some groups use it to force a society backward while countries like France want to remove it from public life in order to better assimilate their sizable African Arab population into their mainstream.

A Christian friend from Baghdad told me that his mother and sisters don't dare go out of the house without a Hijab. They are afraid of abuse by religious zealots or being raped by American soldiers. Women in Iraq have gotten the worst deal out of this occupation-liberation mess.

But Arab women must stand up for themselves and demand their freedom again. Last week a woman in Afghanistan was beheaded in public. She was accused of Zinah or Adultery. I was under the impression that the Taliban regime was removed by America. But I guess "talibanizing" a society does not come from regimes or governments. It is a force stronger than any regime and it is sweeping through the Muslim world like a hurricane.

The Muslim extremists who are championing the "rebirth" of Islam are using the Hijab and the obsessive control of women as weapons of mass destruction. They have hijacked the spirit of Islam and turned it into a set of rules of conduct to be enforced against the Muslim woman.

Of course, Muslim women don't have the guts to say what I have just said. They comply with the rules of a society governed by powerful men. Wearing a Hijab or not wearing it is not the issue. My own mother wears it while my sister is against it. I support both. I support their right to choose. I support freedom of expression.

May 14, 2005

A Simple plan for the Mayor of Detroit

Almost eighty percent of the residents in the city of Detroit are African American. So they should have an African Town. A segment of the city like Mexican Town in Southeast Detroit or Arab Town in East Dearborn. They should have a nice safe place where the streets are decorated with ornaments from their colorful culture and where people sit outside in cafés, and where joy in culture thrives.

That's what I said to an African American friend. He contested that the Mayor of Detroit, Kwame Kilpatrick, vetoed the proposal that was approved by City Council last year. I told him that the Mayor did the lawful thing. He looked at me perplexed and protested that the Arabs have their museums and great big mosques and the Mexicans have their arched buildings and restaurants while Blacks who form the majority of the population in Detroit got no culture.

I told him that the Mayor can not approve an illegal measure even if it were passed by city council. The proposal that was approved used public funding to create a town basically to benefit one segment of the population. It was a racist proposal. Arabic Town and Mexican Town were built by the people and not by public money. I told my friend that the people in Detroit should not wait for city council or the Mayor to do things for them. They need to do things for themselves and to get on with building their city.

The Detroit City Council is waiting for handouts so they can line up the pockets of their friends. I can name so many nice project ideas that never made the light of day. Remember the Empowerment Zone that President Clinton appropriated 100 million dollars for. What became of that money? Where did it go?

The real problem in Detroit lies with incompetent government and rampant crime. Both go hand in hand and one causes the other. It is a vicious cycle to break out of. The bottom line is that most politicians in Detroit are either corrupt or incompetent. And both attributes create the greatest injustice.

This year there are local elections and the residents of Detroit will choose a Mayor. The current Mayor has made many mistakes in the past three years but has also made some gains. The biggest gain is the revitalization of some parts of downtown Detroit. But this Mayor is struggling with a shrinking revenue base and a bloated local government.

Thirty years ago Detroit had over two million people. Now it has a little over 800,000, and the trend continues downward. So why isn't Detroit attracting people? Because of crime. And because there is a helpless local government.

The different candidates vying for the Mayoral position do not offer any real solutions. Sharon McPhail, a Councilwoman, will use personal attacks as a way to discredit the incumbent. Freman Hendrix, a former deputy Mayor, is a bureaucrat who is trying to capitalize on the legacy of former Mayor Dennis Archer. But none really has a grasp over the issues. They are all wallowing in the misery of the culture in Detroit. The culture of entitlements and handouts.

America has no more money to give to inner cities. We have a Republican President whose primary agenda is the Energy and Defense industries. These industries feed on wars and investment in foreign lands, like Iraq. So, Detroit should not expect any handouts from the Federal government for at least the next four years.

The city of Detroit will remain on its own. Unless it makes radical changes to the way it behaves it will continue to trend downward. Changes must be championed by the people themselves. They should

58

not wait for the government to do things for them. I told my black friend to start investing some of his money in the city of Detroit. He said he was too scared to put any of his money in it. Well, if rich black people don't want to invest in Detroit, why should the rest of America give a damn?

But Arabs and Chaldeans have a great economic interest in the city of Detroit. They own the majority of the small businesses that keep the streets alight. They must have a say so in the way Detroit is governed. Their biggest enemies are crime and government.

They fight the criminal elements of insecurity and theft on a daily basis. On top of that, they are raided by inspectors from the Engineering Department who strut like self-righteous peacocks writing "violation" tickets.

It's been almost a year and a half since Mayor Kwame Kilpatrick unleashed the Vice squad of the Detroit Police Department against all Arab and Chaldean stores. They raided their stores, handcuffed people and wrote 1,300 tickets of so called "violations." This mayor must pay the price of that ruthless act that did not benefit Detroit or its people. Now is the time for all Arab and Chaldean small business owners in Detroit to give him a payback, and to make an example of him so that whoever the new Mayor will be, he/she will learn to respect their contribution to the city.

Here's a simple plan for the next Mayor of Detroit. The administration of the Water Department needs to be contracted to a private firm, so that it acts like a respectable utility company that serves a community. One third of the city government employees need to be handed their pink slips, the sooner the better. One third of the Police force needs to go to early retirement for its questionable integrity. No more taxes period. No more hikes in property tax and no more proposals of taxing fast food or gas stations.

The Mayor himself should walk down a Detroit street every day and talk to small business owners on how they can expand their businesses and create a partnership with the Engineering Department. He should sell city-owned vacant properties adjacent to thriving businesses thereby helping them expand. Today, it takes over two years to buy a vacant property from the city of Detroit. That is unacceptable.

Commercial blight that litters the city should be bulldozed and offered to medium size companies in the form of industrial parks.

59

The new Mayor must work to create a culture of life and self-reliance in Detroit. Renewal in Detroit will not happen from the outside. It has to be championed from within and rich black people must believe in their people and begin to invest in them.

May 21, 2005

Exiting Iraq in 30 days

Can America do it, appear victorious and have Iraq as its best ally in the Middle East? Yes, but only if the Bush administration begins to use its brain instead of brawn.

The likely scenario is that it will withdraw from Iraq the same way Syria was forced to withdraw from Lebanon; with its tail between its legs after a prolonged miserable military occupation.

The concept of Democracy is usually built on a desire from within a nation to have the rule of the People. Iraq is being force-fed this concept from the top down. This has not worked from the first day of liberation and continues to be the crux of the problem. American politicians fail to understand this diagnosis because they just don't know how Arab community is naturally organized.

The concept of community in Arab culture is very different from the applied concept in Western nations. Arab society is organized all over the Arab world not around government or around the idea of a nation-state. Arab society orbits around family and it is the nucleus of politics. Heads of families band around a tribal leader who rises as a regional chieftain. The tribal leader is a person who directs the destiny of thousands of people through regular council with heads of families. The idea of council and participation is built-in. It doesn't need the ballot box to make it happen.

Tribal leaders rely on the council of religious clerics who advise them on matters of dispute and how justice can be achieved. Disputes between families rise because of criminal acts. Discussion takes place on the nature of the crime committed and the claims of each party. Evidence is presented and both parties argue their point of view. The tribal leader makes a judgment and it is enforced upon the parties by the power of his reputation in society. Conflicts are resolved through mediation and compromise.

60

Tribal leaders command power over thousands of young men who are ready to go to war to enforce their word. That's the way Arab society has been organized for thousands of years.

On the other hand, the industrial revolution in the West promoted the idea of a nation-state. People moved and migrated from one country to the next looking for a better economic life. America rose as a fulfillment of the nation-state idea. Government in America directs every aspect of a human being's life from the way he uses a toilet to the way he sleeps with his wife.

In America, government has taken over the role of family and it presents itself as the protector of the child from the abuse of his parents. It presents itself as the father of all. In the past sixty years the rise of the welfare system has produced a class in society I call the "children of the state". These are young men and women born out of non-committal relationships and raised mostly by single mothers supported by the state. They are poor but handed out enough crumbs off the table so they are always grateful to the government. They enlist in the army as soon as they reach adulthood and pledge their unswerving allegiance to the Commander-in-Chief.

The children of the state guarantee the power of the state over its own citizens. The children of the state wage wars against other nations and subjugate them to their way of thinking. Colin Powell is a prime example of how the children of the state became the rulers of nations. He was raised by a single poor mother and his hope in life was to join the army so it makes him a "somebody". He ended his illustrious career as a "nobody".

For hundreds of years the Ottoman Empire applied the same concept that America discovered in the twentieth century. The Turkish army used to raid cities and abduct all its children and then raise them in an army boot camp. They were called the "Inkisharia" army. The power of the Turkish state rested in their hands as it still does today.

The concept of community in America orbits around the power of the state to take care of people. The state is the family and that's why Americans are obsessed with the family of a President because it is the first family. There are no celebrated families more than the first family. Most American families dissolve back into the ocean of the state when children reach the age of 18. Children move out to other states and keep a loose relationship with the parents. They call their mothers on "Mothers Day" and they gather if they're lucky during Christmas.

Arab society is a tightly-knit community that existed around the power of family since the beginning of human civilization. It doesn't need George Bush to organize it. In its dealings in Iraq so far, this administration has proven to be either corrupt or grossly incompetent. And both attributes are creating great injustices.

Getting out of Iraq in 30 days is simple. An empowered diplomat from America must go to Iraq and rebuild its civic society from the bottom up. He needs to meet with regional tribal leaders and ask them to create local councils that can govern their areas. These local councils can elect mayors who will collect the trash and run the neighborhood police stations. Tribal leaders will be given the power to enlist young men in an army that reflects the collective will of these chieftains. As each locality is handed over to a tribal council US forces can be moving out of the streets to the outskirts. Judges will be selected by tribal councils and the power of the court can be enforced by the council. The rule of law will evolve from the bottom up and the Constitution will simply be a seal reflecting the union reached.

It's not that hard to figure out. It's simple to do but it needs someone who knows how Arab society works. It needs someone who knows how to give dignity to the dignified leaders of a people.

The Bush administration dismantled the Iraqi army and then disassembled the institutions of government, and now it is tearing Iraqi society apart. It has placed tribal leaders and heads of families on the side and has given all the power to religious clerics. These Imams are now killing each other which will inevitably lead to a religious-based civil war.

Iraq is now headed towards a theocracy like Iran. But Arabs want a secular democracy based on their tradition of organizing society.

May 28, 2005

Peace between America and Palestine

After almost five years of being excluded from the White House, the Palestinians in the form of their President, Mahmoud Abbas, stood in the Rose Garden again. On Thursday, May 26, Abbas and President Bush held a joint press conference inaugurating the formation of a new relationship between the two people.

I must admit it has been a while since I've seen an Arab leader that made me proud. But Mahmoud Abbas made me proud today. He is the product of a genuine commitment to democracy. He is the only leader in the region who was directly elected by his people. He is fluent in English but chose to speak in his mother Arabic tongue. His language was precise and to the point. In Arabic we had gotten used to hearing many words that meant very little especially from the dictators. Abbas presents a new model for an Arab leader. He is a balanced politician whose words are addressed to the people who elected him, even when he speaks to the most powerful leader on earth.

Abbas had no words of anger towards Israel or America. As a Palestinian American I have a deep attachment to all of the components of my identity. First and foremost I am a Muslim. Then my national identity is permeated by a deep faith in the goodness of humanity. I am an Arab. I am a Palestinian and I am an American. Putting all these together has been an especially tough task especially after September 11th. Many of these components were at war with each other and I felt the conflict tearing me from inside.

I love America. I also love Palestine and I cherish being an Arab. Islam had put them all together in one container that can exist in harmony. I am a proud American and today President Bush made me proud of him. He reaffirmed America's commitment to a viable Palestinian state. He drew a close parallel between a Palestinian mother and an American mother and how both wanted their children to live in peace. He brought the two people much closer to each other and began an irreversible process of creating a strategic alliance between the two people. Bush also understands how a leader is molded in the process of a democratic election. He knows that Abbas did not come asking America for a handout. Abbas had created his own legitimacy. He came to the White House as a dignified leader. He did not come to America asking Bush to keep him in power.

Bush executes the collective will of his nation. He paid respect and gave dignity to the dignified leader of the Palestinian people. America has no respect for people or leaders who do not respect themselves first. That's why most Arab leaders will now view Abbas as a threat. But Abbas had already calculated for that possibility. President Bush was the one who made the statement that all Arab nations and leaders must step up to the plate and fulfill their financial obligations to the Palestinian Authority.

Of course it shames me as an Arab to hear an American intervening to tell the fat Sheikhs of the Gulf to pay up their obligations. As a Palestinian, I do believe that I and my people have a rightful claim in the oil that is stored in every Arab land. I also believe that my suffering as well as the suffering of my people was caused more by illegitimate Arab leaders than Israelis.

My grandfather was the generation of Revolution. My father was the generation of Defeat. I am the generation of Victory. And that is inevitable. My children will be the generation of cultural co-existence between Jews and Arabs. I work for the benefit of my children, and in their eyes I see a greater promise than revenge and war. I see pure love for existence.

I despise the language of anger and hate towards Israel. The path to peace requires that we both see what is good in each other and to let go of warmongering. I tell people every day that building things requires incredible diligence and self-discipline while breaking things is very easy. One can build for twenty years and watch all that go away in one day. Destruction is very easy. Just watch little children and see how they can fight all day long unless adults intervene and punish those who are constantly fighting.

War is easy to do. It is no challenge. It is easy to insult other people and denigrate them. It is easy to turn hurt into anger. It is easy to discriminate against others. It is easy to claim self-righteousness. All these emotions belong to excessive self-indulgence. And as humans we love to indulge ourselves. We love to talk about how great we are and how bad other people are. Very few of us do the hard thing of self-criticism.

I look in the mirror every day and I say to myself "who are you and why do you live?"

I live to build things. I have chosen life over death. I have chosen the path to peace between people. I have chosen to love the Jews and to love anyone who claims to be my enemy. I truly believe that my love will overcome all the hatred that comes my way.

But I am no fool and my love is not free. I use it as a force of goodness stronger than any force of darkness. I believe that peace requires love even if it is improper for Presidents of nations to talk that language. Love to me is far from romance. Love is an unbreakable bond between people. Love takes away my choice of imposing a sense of superiority over others. It is a force of equalization. The needier a person is the more love he deserves. That's why we all love children. They are the neediest creatures.

As an Arab American I lived through a period when Arabs hated Americans and Americans hated Arabs. I could not hate myself. I loved myself first and made sure I loved Arabs and loved Americans. Now, I want Arabs to love Americans and Americans to love Arabs. It is a simple request. I can not be at peace with myself unless Arabs love Americans and Americans love Arabs. My identity is both and I am equally proud and privileged to be part of these two great nations.

June 4, 2005

Allah protects the Qur'an

Every successful civilization thrives on decent human values. It is driven by values that are good to all human beings no matter what race, color or ideological persuasion they belong to. The American civilization thrives on the spirit of goodness to everyone and tolerating all human differences.

The spirit of Islam is oneness of humanity. Its values rest on equality and non-discrimination. Unfortunately, there is not one single nation inhabited by Muslims that reflects the spirit of Islam in its laws. Most Muslim nations have laws that reflect entrenched discrimination. Some of them discriminate against women. Others discriminate against other Arabs but most are believers in sectarianism.

But Islam as an ideology is stronger than its practitioners. It has survived the ages because its book is original and its words were the exact words uttered by its great Prophet, Muhammad (May God Bless his soul).

65

It is without a doubt the exact words of Muhammad. There is no other book that exists on earth that is like it. The Bible which comprises the Old Testament and the New Testament was written by a collection of scholars over a period of six hundred years. The Bible contains the same moral values contained within the Qur'an. But the Qur'an is the juice and the essence of the Abrahamic Faith of unity of existence.

Most Arabs who speak the language of the Qur'an do not understand it. So how about the Pakistanis or Afghans or the Indonesians. None of them truly grasps the meanings contained in the Qur'an. The so-called learned Mullahs of Iran or Saudi Arabia propagate the greatest ignorance in the name of Islam. They have no idea of the simple values contained within the Qur'an.

But I don't really blame them because Arabic is not the mother tongue of the majority of Muslims. It rests, as it always has, with us the Arabs to interpret the Qur'an and propagate its values to the rest of humanity. We are the custodians of that book.

I listened intently the other day to an interview on Al-Jazeera TV. Mr. Shakroon was a prisoner held in Guantanamo for three years. He is from Morocco and he was released a few months ago. He described the acts of desecration of the Qur'an by prison guards as "routine" and orderly. He said that it was done all throughout the time he spent there. He could not imagine how these acts were not part of a policy. He said that the prison guards were regimented and closely restricted in their behavior. He added that a prison guard would not allow a prisoner to go to the bathroom unless he checked with his superior. So he concluded that it was prison policy to desecrate the Qur'an. I believe him.

Muslims all across the world demonstrated when this story broke out almost a month ago. I heard that some Muslims in Dearborn wanted to organize a demonstration. I advised against it. I believe that America reflects the spirit of Islam more than the Afghani government or the Pakistani regime. However, there are some bad apples just like Arabs have Osama Bin Laden and his thugs.

These thugs did not learn any lessons from the trials of the Abu Ghuraib prison guards accused of abuse. We, Muslim Americans understand that the greatest majority of Americans are good people who respect other people's religions, books and rituals. By demonstrating in the streets we antagonize these good Americans and

66

we tell them that they are bad like the thugs that work in the prisons. That is not a correct course of action.

So, I urge all American Muslims not to even think about demonstrations. Their result will be the exact opposite thing of what we want. We want these thugs to be made an example of and to be rounded up and tried as a group. There seems to be a concerted policy of abuse in prisons. It is coming from people high up in the Defense Department. The only way to find out how high this policy goes up is by doing hearings in the US Congress and the Senate.

Although Congressman John Conyers has authored a bill to respect the Qur'an we believe that more should be done. I call on our good friend the Dean of the House, Congressman John Dingell to call for hearings in the Congress and to push this matter diligently so that the culprits are all brought to justice.

I also believe that Defense Secretary Donald Rumsfeld has had ample time to fix this problem. He appears to be in a weak position to do anything about it. He appears to be ruled by his underlings and unable to enforce the policy of the White House or the President. Bush came out and stated his position very clearly that his administration abhors such acts. But the White House is not totally clean on this issue. Right from the beginning Mr. Bush opposed subjecting all these detention camps to international law or the Geneva Convention on treatment of prisoners of war. He reserved the exclusive right of his executive office in holding and trying these prisoners.

Till today I have yet to hear of one trial for any of these prisoners. All these things that are taking place in the shadow of darkness do not serve our democracy. All these proceedings shrouded in secrecy and protected by so-called "national security" have hurt us internally and in the eyes of the rest of the world.

I believe that the Bush administration has failed in managing these detention centers. It is time for the Congress to take over and to create an oversight committee that blows these steel gates wide open for all to see. The military has not been a trustworthy custodian of American values.

I find it ironic that Mr. Shakroon now has a chance to defend himself and to try his accusers in the court of public opinion. Why was he detained for 3 years? Why does the Congress of the people remain silent? Do people of other colors and religions not hurt like we do? Is it our policy to antagonize Muslims and make them the enemies of America?

I truly believe that if America intends to reform Arabs and Muslims it has to work harder at reforming itself first. Charity always starts at home.

I never worry about the Qur'an or its values. Allah protects them, now and forever.

June 11, 2005

Re-thinking Community Activism

A good American who distrusts Arabs asked me the other day "will you live and die in America?" I said: what do you mean? He said: will you die and be buried in this country? Without hesitation I answered: absolutely.

I guess I am more American than anything else now. For over twenty five years I have lived off the fruits of this land. I ate its food, drank its water and breathed its air. My composition had mixed with its elements and its people. I have gone through good times, bad times and built this country with blood, sweat and tears.

I always regret that the land I came from never gave me a chance to give. It always refused my effort or tried to enslave me for the measly pennies that business owners in the Middle East always offer their employees.

Last Monday just before midnight it was mayhem on "the Boulevard of Arabia", Warren Avenue in Dearborn. The Detroit Pistons had won the Eastern conference cup and beat the Miami Heat. Hundreds if not thousands of fans were out on the street honking, dancing and partying. Shirts came off and liberated girls hung out of the windows of cars celebrating.

Arabs in Dearborn have melted into the American pot more than appears to the naked eye. They are definitely out of the cocoon and they had emerged with an American spirit. They laugh when America laughs. They cry when America cries and their challenge with substance abuse has become the same challenge that faces America. Their concerns are America's concerns.

68

In the late nineties there was a healthy explosion of Arab American organizations. They reflected the explosion of Arab population in this area. Some offered social services and others worked on empowerment and representation. They have done a wonderful job of shepherding the new immigrants onto the American stage. But participation in these organizations has waned recently. Why is that?

Many leaders of these organizations blame the people for not caring while the people blame the leaders for hogging power. The leaders want to unite the people and make them a strong voice that speaks with one tongue. But many leaders rode the wave of the people and achieved considerable personal gains. The people benefited too. They voted in record numbers in last year's election.

I say more power to the leaders. I really don't blame anyone or discredit any human being for having ambitions and trying to improve his lot in life. Power is created and it is rarely given by the people. In a democracy an aspiring leader wrests power by his/her sheer will power and determination. The people do not give him power at the ballot box. The aspiring leader had already empowered himself when he signed up as a candidate. The more this candidate adopts the views of the majority the higher the likelihood that he will win an election.

I participated in many of these organizations and I am proud to have many of these leaders as my good friends. They are honorable people who do the best they can with the resources available to them.

Every once in a while I receive a phone call from a so-called angry Arab American constituent. He or she tells me to give my leader friend a message. Their message is usually "who put you up there to represent me?" They go on to give me a piece of their mind about how they dislike someone's accent or somebody's looks. Most of the complaints are personal and have nothing to do with community issues.

I listen patiently till all the abusive personal remarks have been released. Then, I turn the table around and tell them "why don't you get involved and do something about your dissatisfaction?". I am used to the answers that follow. I call them the "thousand and one Arabian excuses". One excuse after the other. They flow abundantly and in the end I say: "in the absence of other people this is what you have to live with." That's when they say: I don't want to be an Arab any more.

69

They will say anything to avoid taking responsibility for the collective. They want the leader to be tailor-made and he has to be a Saladin or Jamal Abdel-Nasser. They are not satisfied to have leaders as regular people like they are.

Every immigrant community that came to America has gone through the same growing pains. I choose the African American model as the closest one to the Arab American. They had their civil rights movement in the fifties and sixties. Then, there was the rise of militancy in the early seventies with people like Malcolm X. Then, Jesse Jackson ran for President in 1984 and 1988. He mobilized his community at a national level and raised their political awareness. They became a force to reckon with in the nineties. Most of their leaders began their journey of legitimacy from the church pulpit.

Al Sharpton, Jesse Jackson, Barack Obama and many others obtained their legitimacy directly from the ballot box. The nature of an Arab is not like the nature of a Jew. Many Arab Americans keep referring to the Jewish model as if it would apply to them. Jews are a lot more united in their nature. They have an innate sense of insecurity because of four thousand years of history of persecution. By their nature they will stand together more than Arabs would. Arabs are a very diverse people.

The Jewish lobby in America has achieved tremendous heights. I often admire the synergy of their organizations and the speed of their coordinated actions. It is to their credit that they can advance their issues much more effectively than we ever can.

Our community activism is now at a cross-road. We either follow the Jewish model or the African American or the Hispanic. We need courageous leaders who will step up to the plate and run for national offices. They need to run for US Congress or Senate or Governor of Michigan. Winning the election is not the purpose here.

Or what we need to do is democratize all our organizations. We can create the Congress of Arab Americans and have a dozen or so leaders directly elected by Arab American voters in the tri-county area.

What's important here is to begin re-thinking community activism and come up with fresh ideas that excite our community and keep it moving forward in its journey of empowerment.

70

Chicken dreams in a banana republic

In one of my forays to the Middle East I decided to start a business. I researched and found that the average price of a kilogram of chicken was $1 and I could produce it for less than $0.12. It made good business sense.

I was in a Banana Republic and the real name is irrelevant as it could well be any country in the Middle East, for all intents and purposes. Besides, I still want to be able to go to that country and I am scared of mentioning its name because I have been interrogated by its secret police in a previous adventure. I have seen what they can do to a proud man.

I wanted to build a chicken farm and become the Frank Purdue of Arabia. Building the chicken coup was no big deal. There were plenty of cheap Egyptian laborers that can put up a block building overnight. Bringing water to the god-forsaken piece of land that my family owned proved to be a more challenging task. Finally, I settled on digging a well. It was much cheaper than trying to buy water and truck it over long miles of unpaved barren land.

I found myself going back to the dreaded government agencies that always said No, regardless of the nature of the question. I wanted to do things the right way. I applied for a permit to open up a chicken coup and raise homegrown chicks. They sent me to the health department which sent me to the taxes and revenue department. They in turn sent me to the Ministry of Interior to get a security clearance. I applied for that clearance, put the required stamps on the application and got the required signatures as I toured the corridors of the Secret Police or Al-Mukhabarat fortress. It brought back bad memories but this time I found the staff more helpful and less militant.

They instructed me to come back in a couple of weeks. Meanwhile, one of the Lieutenants in that building liked my fresh approach and can-do attitude. He guessed that I came from America. I told him about my project and we went out to lunch to talk about it. He advised me that I was a "green-horn gringo" who will be eaten up alive in the web of that country's nepotism. He told me to go back to America before I wasted more of my time and money, and begged me to take him to America.

71

I was determined to prove to myself that building a business in the Middle East was as straightforward as it was in America. I had convinced myself that people were helpless because they did not know American business management and marketing techniques. I refused to believe that governments were the source of people's helplessness.

I bought a small stick shift pick-up and began going to the land every day to plan the structures and bond with my chicken dream. I got to know the bedouins who grazed their cattle in the land and they speculated that I would hit water if I dug five meters below. They hated government and they raised their own chicken and lamb without permits or taxes.

But I wanted access to the big city's market. The Ministry of Interior called and referred me to the Ministry of Trade. I was informed that the price of chicken was regulated by the government in order to protect the consumer. No problem. They told me that I would not be allowed to charge retail outlets more than $0.70 per Kilo. The project was still feasible and there was big money to be made in raising chicken.

I went to a small live chicken store in my neighborhood. I picked a live chicken and the attendant killed it and cleaned it for me. He charged me $0.62 per Kilo. I was surprised and asked him where he got his chicken from. He said from a chicken farm. I was pleased that market forces were at play keeping prices even below the government's cap.

I asked the store owner if he would buy my chicken if I ever offered them to him. He said he would not pay more than $0.30 per Kilo. O.K. there was still money to be made in raising chicken. But he could not buy more than a dozen chickens a day.

I went to the supermarket and found that most of the frozen chicken came from Bulgaria and it sold for $0.50 per Kilo. So, I thought I could kill and clean the chicken and then sell it frozen. I asked the Ministry of Trade about frozen chicken and they said there was only one authorized importer of chicken, in order to protect the consumer.

They referred me to the Ministry of Agriculture to inquire about homegrown frozen chicken. There, I was informed that only one licensed facility was authorized in the entire banana republic to do massive chicken slaughter and cleaning operations. I asked for an application to open another one. That's when the bureaucrat raised his eyebrows and said: you have to talk to the Prime Minister about that.

So, I went to the Prime Minister's office but the security guards almost arrested me for trying to get an appointment with him to discuss the chicken situation in the country. I finally came across an elected member of the parliament who waited in line for public transportation in what they called "service" cabs, or taxis where five people shared the fare and the ride.

The "congressman" laughed when I told him about the chicken issue. He informed me that there was a law on the books which gave exclusive rights to one company to operate a chicken slaughterhouse. The company was in partnership with the feudal lords, the so-called high-up politicians, or the real owners of the fabricated republic. He gave me a brotherly advice which stuck in my mind till the day I die. He said you need to find a Sheikh or an Ameer (prince) to be your partner if you want to secure a business in this country.

I asked if he could sponsor a new law. He said: "do you think we have a Parliament like your Congress in America? Here we are not allowed to initiate laws. We only discuss what the prime minister and his government dictates to us."

All my chicken dreams vanished in that taxi. I felt like the rest of the citizens who sat in that car; helpless and will always be helpless and hopeless.

June 25, 2005

Arafat's legacy: Corruption

A Palestinian American merchant got an order from the Palestinian Authority recently for a shipment of American products. He shipped the container and sent the invoice. A couple of weeks later his invoice was sent back and he was told to double the price and to send a new invoice. He was also given instructions on bank accounts he should transfer the extra money to. It is called corruption. Pure and simple. It is happening every day in every Arab regime.

Mahmoud Abbas (AbuMazen), the Palestinian President, who feared for his life while Arafat was still alive, flew to Paris in a hurry with his Prime Minister Ahmad Qureia (AbuAlaa') just before Arafat exhaled his last breath. They negotiated for long hours with Arafat's wife,

Suha, who was waiting to inherit billions of dollars stashed away in accounts all over the world. Of course, the outcome of these negotiations was hushed and till today no one knows what happened to the billions. It is rumored that Suha finally settled for a palace in France and about 500 million dollars in cash. Who got the rest of the money and where is it? Doesn't it belong to the Palestinian people?

Yasser Arafat, may God grant compassion upon his soul in the hereafter, was a corrupt man. He collected billions of dollars at the expense of the misery of his people and he ended up dying as a prisoner of Palestinian misery. His fortune was estimated anywhere between 5 and 15 billion dollars. No one knew the extent of his wealth except his closest confidant and foremost accountant, the current Prime Minister, Abu Alaa'. In the Eighties his gang cornered the banana market in Africa as it operated out of Tunis. They ran multi-billion dollar multinational corporations under the radar of the press or the people.

Of course, Arafat was never accountable to anyone and whoever opposed him he got rid of. History will not be kind to him and definitely he won't be remembered as a hero, if I can help it. Over forty years he squandered one opportunity after the other to lead the Palestinian cause in the right direction. He started a fight with the late Jordanian Monarch, King Hussein and tore the country apart. Jordanians and Palestinians were always one family bound by common ancestral ties. Arafat managed to make cousins kill their own cousins. After that black September of 1970 Palestinians were treated as second class citizens in the country of Jordan where they made up more than 70 percent of the population. But Arafat's damage was always far reaching as he never thought of others, and he was willing to sacrifice the last Palestinian soul for his personal cause.

He got to Lebanon and we told him not to meddle with its internal affairs. But he only listened to his own demons. He built a new empire in Lebanon. It was a reflection of his paranoid angry personality. In the end, the Lebanese people welcomed the Israeli liberators with flowers and old women in the south threw rice at the rolling Israeli tanks in jubilation. I'll never forget that scene as it played on television when I was living in Philadelphia. My Lebanese friends told me their point of view and I remember saying at the time: "we Palestinians deserve everything bad that has ever happened to us but we just don't deserve God's curse of putting Arafat in charge of our fate."

No Palestinian anywhere in the world was safe from Arafat's long arm of destruction. He never built anything positive in his life. He only knew how to destroy other people's lives. So, when the first Gulf war started in 1991 he went to Baghdad and necked with Saddam Hussein. The Iraqis were kicked out of Kuwait and the fat Sheiks came back and all their vengeance was directed at the Palestinians. They threw most of them out and over 400 hundred thousand moved to Jordan penniless.

In 1994 Arafat arrived as a hero in Jericho. I was willing to give him yet another chance at repentance. Shortly afterwards, he set up a company called "Al-Muheet" which literally means "the ocean". He began negotiations with the Israelis on economic autonomy of the soon-to-be liberated Palestinian territories. In Gaza the price of cement was 40 Israeli Shekels per ton before Arafat's arrival. There were many suppliers of cement and there was a healthy competition. It is a known fact that half of the Palestinian economy is fueled by construction activity.

Shortly after Arafat's arrival to Gaza all Israeli cement companies were barred from doing business there. There was only one authorized dealer of cement and it was called "Al-Muheet". The price of cement jumped within the first year to 78 Shekels per ton and there was a waiting line. Al-Muheet thrived and expanded to become the only authorized supplier of fuel and gasoline. Many gas stations began selling out to the new Palestinians who grew up in the diaspora and came back with Arafat. They all came to the "promised land" with a healthy appetite of greed. "Al-Khitiar" (or the old Sheikh) as Arafat was nicknamed promised them that Palestine was going to be the land of milk and honey.

Eventually, Al-Muheet or the Ocean swallowed up the Palestinian economy.

The rest of Arafat's story hurts more to remember but he left a legacy of layers of Palestinian society that sees corruption in government as a normal way of life. Internal reform in a nation is far more important than any external threat. Internal reform is not a one time deal. It is the set up of a system of checks and balances whereby the Congress of the people holds the Executive Branch accountable. It has the right to investigate and to change things, policies and people. Internal reform mechanisms define the way a nation views itself. That's why in this country the fight for civil rights, individual liberties and equal opportunity is of great importance. Once America changes the way it views its own citizens it will change the way it behaves towards foreign nations.

The phrase "Internal Reform" in the Middle East has been adopted by the corrupt politicians and they are corrupting American politicians. American values are proving to be too weak in the face of the feudal system of corruption in the Middle East.

Our local Palestinian American merchant who abided willingly by the Palestinian Authority's "way of doing business" was rewarded by an offer to go to Palestine and become a deputy Minister in the government of Abu Ala'a.

Arafat's legacy of corruption is like an Aids virus and it has spread throughout the body of Palestine.

July 2, 2005

Arab Society is broken

I remember the days of puritan activism when Arabs were still a novelty in America and whenever I told somebody that I was an Arab they asked me right away if my father owned an oil well. Those were the good old days when Americans thought of us as people who lived in tents, rode camels and pumped a barrel or two of oil a day. And oh the harems. That was always my favorite part. I told them that I already had a tent-full of them and they awaited my return to the Sahara eagerly.

There was a time when we were only a handful in this country and whenever we got together we staged a demonstration. We loved to demonstrate and did not care about acceptance, public opinion or the reckless statements we made to the media.

I remember once in 1982, Maer Kahane was giving a lecture to his ardent supporters in Philadelphia, where I had lived. I went to the hall with a handful of my buddies and we heckled him at every racist remark he made. The mostly Jewish audience was so annoyed with us that they attacked us and literally carried us out of the hall and threw us in the street. I loved it even as I wiped my bloody nose. It made me feel that I was one man who made a difference.

Then, we staged our own events at the University and formed GUPS (General Union of Palestine Students). We became organized in our approach and we held debates with very smart Jewish professors who later gave us bad grades. Then, we moved on to politics and helped Walter Mondale and Geraldine Ferraro in 1984 in their presidential campaign.

Most of us went on to the business world where we knew we could make a real difference and apply our individual initiative to create something of lasting value. Then, Arab American organizations began to spring up and we supported them. Then, September 11th happened and we were no longer the "camel jockeys". All of a sudden we became "hijackers and terrorists".

Most of us who do not really seek acceptance from Americans were not bothered by the new stigma. We'd been used to it all our lives and we knew how to stand up for ourselves on an individual basis.

We are not a weak people as individuals. Our identity is not a reaction to Israeli occupation or to the false perceptions of many Americans. We are a peace-loving people who simply seek fairness in life. We came to America running from wars and dictatorships.

We want to heal America and mend its relationship with Arabs. Our selfish objective in life is to eliminate wars and dictatorships in the Middle East. They have been the source of our misery all along. These simple objectives are further out of reach today than they were twenty years ago. War rages in the heart of the Arab world and the dictators and their royal highnesses are more entrenched in power than ever before. Why do we keep sliding backward?

We lived through the ignorance of the dark ages of the Ottoman Empire for four centuries and then emerged as an illiterate, bare-footed hungry people. Our hunger and starvation in World War I led to massive waves of immigration out of the Middle East. We roamed the earth looking for a new home. Many of us who became very wealthy in foreign lands still behaved like they were so hungry. And so all we cared about in the past one hundred years is feeding our ever growling stomachs and making more babies.

Arab society is tribal in nature and most Arabs despise even the idea of government. Islam came to turn all these warring tribes into a pluralistic society. It succeeded for a little while and the Arab nation became a beacon of light for humanity. Then, the Ottoman Turks abolished public education for hundreds of years and Arabs went back to their pre-Islam nomadic and pagan ways.

In the late Twentieth century there was a resurgence of Islam as Iran led the way with its revolution. But they misunderstood Islam and turned it into a centralized religion controlled by a ruling class of clergy. Then, people began to take up the new message of fundamentalism. Men grew their beards, women covered their heads and faith turned into a repressive set of strictly enforced rituals. All the while the great Muslim values of human rights, liberty and equal opportunity were lost in the distortion.

Now, Islam is mostly concerned with repressing women in society and justifying why they are lesser human beings. Bearded Arab men argue all day long on Arabic TV's why man is superior to woman and that the only role for women in life is to be in the kitchen and to make babies. They quote verses from the Qur'an which they do not comprehend.

Regular Arab men believe the words of the bearded ones. So they rarely invest in the education of their daughters and when they do they want them to sit at home after they had earned a higher degree. Anywhere an unmarried girl goes she needs to report to her mother or brothers where she is and what she is doing. Most of the conflicts that rage between families emanate from a dispute over women.

It is normal for an Arab household to have the father as the ultimate dictator who allows little leeway for negotiations or discussion. Then, we wonder why all our societies are ruled by dictators and despots. There is no mystery.

Our political regimes in the Middle East are built on principles of inequality and hypocrisy. Then our dearly beloved organizations here in America began cozying up to these regimes. A few years back they tested us by bringing an obscure prince to be honored at a banquet. We did not say anything for the sake of "Arab unity". And so they were emboldened by the absence of our protestation and began bringing the heads of regimes to be honored. They opened the Arab museum here in Dearborn last month, and brought the head of the Arab League; Amer Mousa to be a guest of honor. We had become another Arab country in exile and we should get a seat in the Arab League.

Earlier this month, the ADC in Washington brought Saudi Prince Al-Walid Bin Talal, honored him and milked him for Six million dollars. We don't need their money and we don't need their corruption. We need them out of power and that's the only message our organizations should take to them.

The Arabian Dream

Recently I completed the making a non-fiction film about Arab Americans. I called it "The Arabian Dream" and it is a tale about Arab Americans. I started marketing the movie almost a month ago by placing it in different film festivals, getting it screened by different groups and making contacts with distributors to show it in theaters.

The making of a non-fiction movie was an eye-opening journey. I was threatened by lawsuits, chased by cops, and solicited by ministers and prostitutes in the streets of Detroit. I approached a drug dealer on a street corner one time and when he detected the lens of the camera he whipped his pistol out. I survived.

I found out that when you are shooting unscripted real life the lens of the camera begins to act as the eye of God. It records people's good deeds and bad deeds. Most people are introverted and camera shy. They truly believe that they live in a bubble, and what they are doing, even though it is in the light of day, is unseen and unrecorded by anyone.

My lens caught a Dearborn policeman enforcing his own Iraqi or Israeli-style military check point on Chase Road. His car was parked on the side and he was standing in the middle of the road just flagging cars down and asking for people's identification cards. My lens went across the street and zoomed in on the scared Arab faces sitting behind the wheel. He saw me and quickly ran across the street towards me. He asked what I was doing as if I had committed a crime and it was time to confess. I lowered the camera and he figured it stopped rolling. He asked for my Id which I refused to give because I suspected he would charge me with something.

He had an angry and loud voice and just barked words at me while his lips trembled. I knew the man was unstable and I told him that I was a tourist from California and it was my hobby to take pictures. I retreated in a hurry giving him little chance to engage. I went to the end of the road and hid out of sight. I caught people at the traffic light and asked them why he was stopping them. None of them would agree to a camera interview while they were incensed by the mistreatment. In my mental notes I recorded: they deserve what they get.

I wanted to crack the vault of secrecy of Arab society and show it the way it is, with no filters or explanations. I go to the mosque regularly and I pray the Friday "Jama'a" or group prayer. One time I took my small camera with me and kept it in my pocket as I usually did, in case something interesting happened on the stage of real life.

A Taliban look-alike long bearded Imam from Egypt was shouting his sermon at the sleepy congregation in broken English. I went into my usual trance ignoring the words as most people did. Then, his words got interesting. He was calling America the enemy of Islam and all Muslims in the world. I took the camera out and crawled up closer to the pulpit.

The lens cap was off and the eye of God was recording the sermon. He saw me and switched to Arabic. He talked for the next twenty minutes thinking that my tape would run out or I would get tired of recording all the worn-out regurgitated lines. I lowered the camera and he switched back to English. He continued blasting the immorality of America, the evil of its repressive foreign policy and painting the war on terror as the latest crusade.

I admired his honesty, audacity and courage. Then, we prayed. I left the hall quickly but he chased me. He demanded the tape and began to frisk me physically looking for that elusive tiny camcorder. My voice became firm as I signaled preparedness to defend myself. Other people jumped in and separated us. "Management" asked to have a word with me. We convened and talked. A couple of other Imams joined in.

I told them that if they were afraid of the consequences of their words, then they should not be saying them. They said that they were not afraid but I was not authorized to record the sermon. I argued that the sermon was given to the public and it belonged in the public domain. They made it clear that they did not want the contents of that tape to fall in the "wrong hands". I assured them that I would polish their image and make them look good in the eyes of America. We made up, kissed and hugged. I made them look good in the movie. But I recorded another mental note: these people have no honor. They'll never stand behind their words.

Then I recorded countless hours of interviews and community events. I began receiving phone calls from people who regretted what they said. A businessman asked me not to use the comments he made about crime in Detroit. He was afraid his business might suffer. I did the story and I made stronger comments myself.

Another notable figure in the community did not want any of the comments he made concerning blight, helplessness and incompetence in the local Detroit government to be shown any where.

I did a lot of interviews and I waded through these long-winded interviews trying to find a common thread. They all said the same thing but could not say it in one clear sentence. In a roundabout way they blamed America for the events of September 11th.

I produced a nice colorful booklet describing the objectives of the film and how it would benefit Arab Americans directly. I sent it to everyone who claimed to be a "somebody" in the community. They patted me on the back and gave me "attaboys". I took this goodwill to the bank but I could not cash it.

Unfortunately, our community has little belief in the power of the media.

July 16, 2005

Homegrown Terrorists

Imagine this scenario. It is January 2006 and the nation's eyes are on Detroit as crowds descend from all over to watch the SuperBowl. Over a hundred thousand people are packed in the new stadium downtown. The game begins the crowds are cheering and then boom an explosion rocks the place. Dark smoke fills the air and the smell of death and destruction quickly sinks into the heart of the crowd. A whole section of the stadium collapses killing thousands.

Terror has struck again in the heart of America and next door to the largest concentration of Arabs living outside of the Middle East; right here in Dearborn. Two days later the authorities pinpoint the terrorists and the FBI raids hundreds of houses in Dearborn.

The authorities find out that the terrorists were US citizens, and they were born and raised in Dearborn. A catastrophe hits Arab Americans in Dearborn.

This scenario is similar to what happened in London last week. The terrorists that struck the underground trains and buses are British Muslims. I spent some time in England and I visited its well

81

established Muslim community. They have mosques all over the country from London to Birmingham to Leeds. They are mostly Pakistani who began immigrating to England over a hundred years ago. In this country when they say the word "minority" the image of an African American comes to mind. In Britain whey they say "minority" people instantly think of the "Paki". They are a large community almost 4 million people representing about ten percent of the population.

London is a center for free Arab media and literally hundreds of publications are found on the newsstands of Edgeware Road, nicknamed "little Arabia". Muslims and Arabs in England are a strong community compared to the presence of Arabs in America. They are rich and powerful. They all stood in solidarity with the government of Tony Blair and with the British people.

Incidents of backlash from the public have so far amounted to firebombing a couple of small mosques and some shattered windows. They are still miniscule compared with the backlash that Arabs faced after 9/11 in America.

The fact remains that these terrorists were homegrown. This is a new creature. Terrorism experts in Europe and America are studying this new phenomenon. We should also pay close attention to it as we will be under the microscope very soon.

Palestinian terrorists are political desperados that see salvation in death. Iraqi terrorists are anarchists gone wild. Saudi terrorists (Bin Laden and his gang) are schizophrenic paranoid Muslims obsessed with covering women from head to toe. These new homegrown creatures from England, what's their beef?

There is no political repression in England and there is no poverty that leads to revolution. Did these Muslim terrorists blow themselves up to go to heaven? I think if they experience some of the hell that they had left behind, especially for their own families, then most likely they are checking into the Hell Motel, right about now. They will stay there forever.

A homegrown terrorist will make authorities focus on us. I suggest that we focus on ourselves before others do, and before we have little choice in the matter, and before our Muslim American homegrown "terrorist-in-waiting" begins to get ideas from the London episode.

In my column last week, I narrated a short story about filming an Imam here in Dearborn giving a sermon "blasting the immorality of America, the evil of its repressive foreign policy and painting the war on terror as the latest crusade." A radio talk show host called me and asked me to explain myself when I said "I admired his (the Imam's) honesty, audacity and courage."

I said: "I admire people when they give you the straight talk to your face. I detest people who say something to your face and something else in your back. I thought this Imam had honor and he was ready to stand behind his words. But he physically attacked me after prayers to confiscate the tape. He was afraid that the tape would fall in the "wrong hands." So basically he was afraid of the FBI. He was not afraid of God, me or the crowd of people who filled the mosque. He turned out to have no honor. I did not admire his ideas or his anger or his hate."

Our Imam was a hypocrite, as I must confess many Imams are, unfortunately. There are a few good ones out there. But most need to be strapped to a barber's chair and have their beards shaved off. Maybe it will break their rigid mold, make them laugh a little, and maybe they'll just turn human with their repressed wives.

Many of these Imams abuse the right of free speech in America by preaching hate. We ignore them thinking that they will somehow go away. But they don't. They get emboldened instead and they tell us how sinful we are in the eyes of their Allah while we sit there like dummies trying to fall asleep. There are some eccentric young men that listen to these parasitic Imams. These Imams make them believe that they have been disfranchised and that their religion calls them to sacrifice.

Such young men exist in every community and in every culture. They don't need to be labeled "Muslim" to take up the call of anarchy, destruction and terror. But this would be a disaster indeed if they begin to take up this call here in our midst. We need to stop this "homegrown" phenomenon before it ever has a chance of taking place. We need to round up all our Imams and re-educate them or turn them over to the FBI. They are the source of these hateful and destructive ideas. They need to learn how to preach opportunities for peace and the culture of life. They need to learn Islam.

As a community we need to protect our self before the protection of Big Brother is enforced upon us. We need to make hard choices in order to avert looming disasters. We came to America running away from war and tyranny. It is time we took concrete steps to correct this imbalance in every aspect of our broken Arab society.

I truly believe that America is humanity's best hope. Here, we will make our final stand and we will stand on the right side of history and reclaim our faith and our humanity. We have not been good salespeople of American values because they've been hijacked by a few extremist Republicans. But, make no mistake about it, our political discourse stems from our love for America.

July 30, 2005

Vicious circles of hypocrisy

I was at a comedy club in Dearborn the other night. The only Arabs present were this writer and his big brother. The comedian was going through his routine and he got to ethnic jokes. He stereotyped blacks, then white Rednecks and of course got to the Arabs. He did a couple of jokes and they were in good taste. Then, he got hung up on the Arab gas station attendant.

He joked: "Turn the pump on I shouted, but all I got was hand gestures. I shouted again turn the pump on and this time he came out and said No English, No English. This is the Midwest and these people come from the Middle East, all I want to know is how did they get here? How did these people get here?". I shouted from a dark corner of the crowded hall: "the same way you got here buddy."

"I don't want to offend any Arabs here but the attendant came out the second time and he shouted at me Yalla hala hala Allah Khala Akber, so how did these people from the Middle East get to the Midwest?". This time I stood up and answered in an engaging way: "the same way you got here buddy. Maybe you need to check your hearing aid but I think you have crossed the line and this is Dearborn. You might get away with this routine in Arkansas but not here my friend."

No one was laughing any more. He cut his routine and moved on to another subject. Ten minutes later I went to the bathroom and there was a speaker in the bathroom that transmitted his dialogue. Maybe he did not realize that. He went on "this is America and this guy should learn to relax and laugh at himself just like we do. If he can't take a joke he shouldn't be here. I am sorry if I offended anyone but let's talk

84

about airport profiling. I don't mean to sound racist but little old ladies did not hijack airplanes and blow them up." I skipped washing my hands as I felt blood boiling in my veins. I ran out of the bathroom and walked deliberately to the center of the floor and addressed the audience.

I said: "people who live in Dearborn remember the days of Orville Hubbard when you got stopped DWB, Driving While Black, this went on for years. Sure he protected white Americans from blacks but he did more damage than good. He supported the sickness in society. Profiling never worked and it will not work now. I don't really appreciate anyone talking behind my back and I do admire your courage saying what you just said here in the heart of Arab America. But if you have something to say to me don't wait till I went to the bathroom to say it. I am totally relaxed. You are the one who is sweating and I do enjoy good humor. So please stick to comedy and everyone will enjoy the show."

At this point, the comedian realized he was in danger of losing the floor and knew he did not tangle with a gas station attendant. He backed off and switched to another subject.

Hypocrisy is something that makes my blood boil. But society is so full of it. Why is the war on terror failing miserably? Because of the vicious circles of hypocrisy that spin people around on a wild ride. They are at play today more than ever before. Everyone wants to pander to the sickest feelings that people have because it simply sells. It makes the nightly news more sensational, Hollywood movies more entertaining and Sunday church sermons more attention-grabbing.

No one is preaching reconciliation, peace, love and understanding. It simply doesn't sell in the media. No one is talking about causal-effects of policies and governments.

How many Arabs sympathized with the Kuwaitis when Saddam and his looting army invaded that banana republic in 1990? I dare to say none that I knew. Why is that? Because the small club of Kuwaiti citizens abuses the larger club of "visiting" employees and treats them like slaves. There is no equality. There is no rule of law for non-citizens. Discrimination and racism is the norm. Who is this "visiting" employee? He is mostly Pakistani, Sri Lankan, Egyptian, Syrian, Lebanese and some Palestinians. It is pretty much the same story in the rest of the oil-rich gulf. The entire free world went to war in 1991 to re-install the fat sheikhs of Kuwait. The free world said that the fat sheikhs are the legitimate owners of Arab oil.

Why is it so hard for Americans to understand that the war on terror is political in nature and not theological. A bunch of poverty-stricken people across the Muslim world have been repressed by their corrupt regimes for at least the last seventy years. These corrupt regimes are propped up today by US foreign policy. If we preach freedom then we must simply cut off these regimes and leave them to the will of their people. These countries were fabricated in the first place by Western powers. The US fabricated Saudi Arabia in 1923. Britain fabricated Kuwait in 1961, as it fabricated many other banana republics like Iraq, Jordan and Egypt. France fabricated Lebanon and Syria. These are all hypocritical fabrications and terror is likely to continue and escalate till we begin believing in freedom ourselves.

The regular Muslim Imam in the Arab world preaches against the policies of the United States and urges Jihad against its brainchild, Israel. At the end of the month he gets his paycheck from the government. He is paid to preach against the US and Israel. His sermons strengthen the illegitimate government that is cozy with the White House. The state of perpetual war keeps politicians relevant in the Middle East. All the while a handful of fat sheikhs pocket the billions of dollars coming from oil. This wealth belongs to all Muslims because Allah did not put oil under Mecca for the benefit of the Saudi tribe. All of these fabricated banana republics need to be canceled out, the sooner the better. That's the way we will win the war on terror.

America, Britain and France need to dismantle all the banana republics that they created in the Middle East, in the twentieth century. It is just that simple.

Please name one US foreign policy that has benefited the repressed hungry man on the Arab street? I can't think of one.

August 6, 2005

Healing the heart of Dearborn

Right after the July 7 attacks in London a throng of British reporters descended on Dearborn. They were interested in the story of Muslims, not necessarily Arabs, because their terrorists were Pakistanis, and how they can coexist with Western culture.

As I shepherded one British journalist around Dearborn, the city of harmony, it felt like a déjà vu. Their July 7th is like our September 11th. I heard the same questions posed to us almost four years ago. I listened to some of the same arguments that accentuated differences and whipped up sentiments so that every Muslim looking person became "suspicious". British Muslims are now facing a backlash similar to the one we endured.

"Yes, we have a sickness in our society", I admitted to many journalists. I don't believe in defensive postures and running away from responsibility. Osama Bin Laden was an Arab and I am an Arab. He is part of my people regardless of how much I condemn or say that he does not represent us or belong to us. I try to own up to the problem and take responsibility. We have a sickness called religious extremism which goes against the spirit of Islam and its holy book, the Qur'an. It is borne out of ignorance piled upon the poverty-stricken masses, which are drowning in hopelessness under the yoke of repressive political regimes.

Our political development has been retarded and our people have not given anything noteworthy to the human civilization in over five hundred years. Our society places little value on the power of the media or intellect. No democracy can ever flourish without heated debates, open discussions and an independent media.

But I also believe that our sickness has a partner. We could not have developed this sickness without the help of western powers. They were only interested in the oil and nothing else. So, they carved up our land into banana republics and appointed corrupt fat sheikhs as custodians of their interest.

Does Bush want democracy or oil from the Middle East? It is a question that is being asked by many lawmakers as they ponder US foreign policy. I have not seen tangible evidence yet that the US is interested in democratizing the Middle East. Cosmetic changes have yet to address the heart of the issue; who owns the Arab oil? The fat Sheikhs or the Arab people? Whoever owns the resources will always own fate and destiny.

We can only heal our sickness through a real partnership with America. We can re-educate our youth about their faith and re-program their minds towards excellence. At the same time we need America to propagate hope by exerting real pressure on every regime in the Middle East to enact real reforms or be subject to sanctions.

Most people in our "little" community here believe that we can not make any changes in the Middle East. They don't realize that what happens in the Middle East has a direct link to our lives here. We're no longer separated. Hatred of America in the Middle East means hatred of Arabs on the streets of Dearborn.

Some of these people choose to cozy up to the illegitimate regimes, accepting money from them, and creating economic forums as a solution. Why not ask some of these regimes to change some of their repressive economic policies to create equal opportunity?

"Are you Muslim first and then American?", the British journalists asked many of the people they met in Dearborn. I answered: "faith transcends national boundaries and countries. We have a deep faith in the goodness of humanity and we find the system in America more consistent with the principles of Islam than in any country where Muslims live. America is a nation of immigrants and its economic system does not afford the luxury of hatred to anyone. Everyone must sell his product or idea to survive. Arabs come to the land of opportunity to make a dignified livelihood and they become more American than anything else."

So, in the eyes of the rest of the world Dearborn shined as a star; a model of harmony and co-existence between Islam and the West. Yes, to the outside world I will defend Dearborn as a model of social harmony and a beautiful garden where diversity bears the best of fruits for humanity.

Relatively speaking, our existence here in Dearborn is far more integrated and assimilated into the American mainstream than Muslims in Britain. I spent some time working in England and listened to the claims of discrimination that Pakistani workers suffer from. The British people do not want to integrate Muslims into their society. It is similar to the struggle of the civil rights movement and welcoming African Americans to live in predominantly white neighborhoods. It hasn't happened yet.

But Arabs are still the lower hand here in Dearborn. We are taxed equally but we have unequal representation and therefore unequal distribution of public resources. A few years ago the basketball courts disappeared from Ford Woods Park, on Greenfield and Ford. I asked why and people whispered to me "to keep the black kids out."

Then, two years ago the park was shut down and millions of dollars were spent on renovating it. All the soccer fields disappeared and now there are three baseball fields. I asked why and people whispered to me "to keep the Arabs out."

Let's face it; baseball is not the dominant sport in non-American culture. I used to play soccer in that park and the game has grown in popularity all over America. Does it make sense that only in Dearborn Soccer has not gained popularity? No. I go to Canton and I see soccer fields replacing abandoned baseball fields and white Moms watching their neatly uniformed girls playing soccer.

In Dearborn, Arabs experience underhanded malicious discrimination practiced in the form of exclusion. The people who hate us are not courageous enough to say it to our face. They just can't help our presence here and they can not deny the goodness that we had created in this town. They want it both ways. They want their property values to go through the roof but they don't want to mix with us.

The good news is that these people form a small but powerful minority. They belong to the past and not to the future of Dearborn.

Whenever I drive on Greenfield in the evening my heart is saddened. Discrimination had turned a park full of life into a deserted baseball field, using our own tax money to light up empty green grass till ten o'clock every night. It's a shame how much destruction discrimination can cause.

August 13, 2005

Liberty for Palestinians

Liberty for the Palestinians has always been the issue. The word "occupation" does not mean much to Americans because they've never been occupied. The war of independence was about taxation without representation.

We don't celebrate Liberty Day or Freedom Day. We celebrate Independence Day on the fourth of July. The British never occupied America because the early colonists were mostly English and

89

European. One can not occupy himself. Therefore, there must be a foreign element involved in occupation. European Jews immigrated to Palestine with the intention to establish a state just for Jews. That is called Zionism. It is the displacement of the original inhabitants of the land with another people.

Occupation is enforced by a foreign army against the will of the legitimate owners of the land. The foreign army occupies cities by building police stations in city centers with big jails barricaded by high fences and barbed wire. The occupied people do not have the right to go to a court to contest the confiscation of their homes or their land. The occupied people do not have the right to bear arms to defend themselves when soldiers shoot at them with M-16's. The occupied people do not have a single political choice that determines their destiny. The occupied people are slaves subject to the will of their masters; the foreign soldiers.

The regime of occupation is enforced by a military commander who sets up check points on every major road and requires the occupied people to carry an identification paper issued by his soldiers. This ID paper is a privilege and a recognition that a person exists as a valid slave.

My family lived in Ramallah in 1967. After the war we were forced out of our home at gunpoint and put on a dump truck and transported to Jordan. We attempted to sneak back to our home as we did not find the refugee tents too comfortable. We did not like being beggars waiting in line for a handout of wheat and sugar. We did not like being bare footed. We did not like sleeping on top of each other in a tent with no plumbing or air-conditioning. We really hated it when it rained and we had to sleep on muddy ground. It was not nice.

My father borrowed money from relatives and bought a small VW bug. One day, before the crack of dawn he woke us up and packed the family of seven into the tiny car. He drove up North and crossed the low Jordan River near the town of Nablus in the Galilee. We were back on the road to Ramallah. People warned us about the many army checkpoints. We did not know what to expect. But we were so happy to be back in our land. On the road we sang, joked and played. I was only five years old but I remember every moment of that drive like it happened yesterday.

Some water had leaked into the car when we crossed the low river. Then, we came upon a traffic jam. All cars just stood still and we waited in the early morning sun for a couple of hours. We got to a military checkpoint. There were tanks and many mean looking soldiers with lots of guns and hats. My father had a pleasant smile for everyone even the soldier who shouted at him asking for papers in broken Arabic. My father showed him his driver's license but the soldier was asking for the "ID". Well, we did not have one and we could not tell him that we just smuggled ourselves back into our own country.

In the eyes of the soldier, it was now his country and we were unwanted pests. He let us through and we were back on the road again. In less than fifteen minutes we hit another roadblock. We waited and then we reached another camp full of soldiers. This time my mother volunteered to chat to our interrogator, and she was so nice to him. She told him that we were visiting some relatives in Nablus and we got stuck there when the war broke out. He bought the story.

The distance was less than sixty kilometers but it felt like a drive across the universe. It was early afternoon when we got to the outskirts of Ramallah and I could smell the sweet aroma of my secure home. My mother had instructed all the kids to tell the same story that she had been telling. We hit another checkpoint. We waited our turn. There was a big soldier with a long red beard asking questions. I was petrified. My mother gave him the usual story but he was not buying. He looked inside the car, stared at the wet carpet, and told me to get out. He took me to the side and lifted me up with one hand like I was a chicken about to be strangled. He shouted at me and said: "you just came from Jordan, didn't you?" I said: "yes" and my words mixed with the salty taste of tears that dripped down my cheeks uncontrollably.

He pointed his large rifle at my father and ordered him to get out. He told him to put his hands up above his head and to go stand in a fenced area. Then, he got everyone out of the car and he told another soldier to take the car. We stood in a fenced area guarded by a younger soldier. We stayed there for hours sweltering in the heat of the July sun. Finally, a big dump truck arrived and we recognized it. We were put on it and sent back over the Jordan River. Back to the valley of death that was full of white tents.

Thirty eight years later and I still can't forget the stench of human flesh that was packed in that dump truck like sardines. I can never erase that from my memory. I cried because I caused my family to become refugees. My father comforted me and told me: "for as long as you live keep telling the truth."

We tried for many years to obtain that precious "ID" card. The application was always denied. The masters would not accept us as slaves and let us back into their plantation. We applied to be free men everywhere we went in the Arab world, but no one accepted our application.

In two weeks the Israeli army will leave the Gaza strip and let go of the Palestinian slaves there, after 38 years of torment. It is a big thing. It is a cause for great celebration. Liberty from the foreign master had finally arrived for some Palestinians.

August 20, 2005

History of Democracy

A 90-year old lady complained to me the other day that her library card was checked by the government. She reads books that could be labeled as "liberal." Most books that offer real education are liberal since they liberate the mind and enlighten it with real knowledge. But ever since the enactment of the PATRIOT Act older people have had nightmares of the prospects of a neo-McCarthyist era. They remember very well the witch hunt of Senator Joseph McCarthy in the 1950's with his buddy; the FBI's notorious J.Edgar Hoover. They hunted down writers, artists, thinkers, politicians, labor union leaders and anyone whom they deemed "un-American". They held public trials in the Congress, sentenced some people to jail and deported others. The great comedian/filmmaker Charlie Chaplin fled the country when they issued a warrant for his arrest. He spent the last twenty years of his life in Switzerland and died "unAmerican" in 1977.

My friend recalls the days of McCarthy and Hoover like they happened yesterday. Her husband had read a book in 1952 that was labeled "subversive" by the FBI. She told me that for many months he could not get a good night sleep because he laid awake at night shaking in fear. He expected men in black to come knocking on his door to arrest him. She asked me: "is the PATRIOT Act bringing those dark days back?"

I told her: "the PATRIOT Act is the last breath of dictatorship in America. It's all over. We had to pander to the fear that swept over the country after September 11th but America, thank God, has become like a rubber band. It snaps back to the center."

American society is driven by a centrist ideology. It is the product of the great partisan warfare that rages constantly in Washington. Many people decry "partisanship" and they claim that nothing ever gets done in Washington because of gridlock and partisan bickering. I thank God for this partisanship and the great debates that take place in our Congress.

Conservatives got a big boost after September 11th and Republicans became the majority party in the US Congress, the Senate and of course the White House. They took the country as far to the right as they can go. But it's all over now. The American people are tired of Tarzan-like politicians beating on their breasts but can not manage a small country like Iraq.

The fact is democracy on this earth is still in its infancy. Some people still think that some information is subversive to the mind and that we should control the kind of information that people can access. Of course, I agree that pornography and sexually explicit material should not be in the hands of children. But democracy feeds on ideas and the open exchange of information. We are talking about political ideas here. The politics of the war on terror for example is costing our country its most precious resources. Our democracy demands a lot more ideas than the worn-out theories put out by retired political operatives who just want to capitalize on their name recognition.

The invention of the internet and the explosion of accessibility to information have made the idea of "monitoring" information infeasible. Libraries themselves are a thing of the past. It is only a matter of time that these buildings will shut down.

Our democracy is still a works-in-progress. Our constitution took eleven years to ratify and another one hundred years to implement the notion of equality. Mankind was created through an evolutionary process over millions of years and finally about fifty thousand years ago we rose from the earth and looked up to the heavens for answers. Creationism as told by the Bible is not in conflict with the ideas of Darwin's scientific evolution.

What is in conflict here is our understanding of the heavenly messages and the inspirational advocacy of people we call prophets like Abraham, Moses, Jesus and Muhammad. Their message was about the oneness of humanity and aligning our political organizations to behave like nature does.

Mankind started on the path of oneness through choosing peace instead of war. People had to learn to trust each other as they created villages near rivers where everyone worked tilling the land. They farmed the land and ate from it. The Greeks invented the first idea of Democracy; which means people or the rule of the people. They went to war over a woman named Helen and destroyed everything. Then, the Romans adopted the idea at the lower local level.

Abraham's theology kept gaining ground and Jesus called for reforming Jews from their rampant excesses. A few hundred years later his followers established the Byzantine Empire which made Christianity the official ideology of the state. The phase of Ideological wars began about 1700 years ago. Then, came Muahmmad in the Sixth century declaring that he was the final prophet of the Abrahamic faith.

He was the descendant of Ishmael, Abraham's first son. Abraham's second son Isaac had claimed the legitimacy of his father. His descendants included prophets like Moses and Jesus whose followers labeled themselves in later centuries as Christians and Jews. Muhammad came with the original spirit of Abraham's message and reclaimed the legitimacy that was denied to Ishmael. His ideology was universal for all people and it wasn't named after him or after a party of people. Islam is not a noun like the word Christianity. It means following a value system aligned with the natural processes of existence. It simply means following the idea of peace. Every man of peace is a Muslim. It spread like wild fire because no one was excluded from Abraham's message of equality.

In the eleventh and twelfth century people fought in the name of the cross and became Crusaders in the holy land. Then, the Turks in the name of Islam pushed deep into Europe and stopped in Bosnia.

Three hundred years ago the economic wars began. People moved from farms to factories as the industrial revolution began. They dreamed of financial independence as the heaven or the ultimate salvation. Dictatorial systems like Capitalism and Communism were invented to manage massive economies. Democracy took a back seat and watched people kill each other over land and natural resources.

Our commercial democracy is finally starting to tilt towards democratic values. We still don't elect our leaders especially the president. We simply have a choice to select between powerful names appointed by industry to uphold the values of capitalism. The War on Terror and the war in Iraq are the final conflicts. They represent an era that humanity will soon bury in its forgotten annals as it chronicles the history of democracy.

August 27, 2005

When Gas goes up Presidents go down

In the past few weeks gas prices went through the roof. I remember less than a month ago when people were complaining so much about the $2.15 price per gallon. Then King Fahd of Saudi Arabia died and within three days gas prices shot up to $2.75 per gallon for regular unleaded. Prices seem to like this new lofty height where they had landed. Or maybe they are just taking a small break to catch their breath before they start climbing yet another steeper hill.

They used to tell us in America politicians do not tinker with God, Gas and taxes. They are the American voters' sacred cows. If a politician touches any of these holy things his career goes to hell. But President George W. Bush has defied all political norms and has violated all the sacred cows while still enjoying himself at the Texas ranch.

In 1973, Saudi King Faisal bin Abdul-Aziz used the weapon of Arab oil as an economic sanction against the West. He stopped pumping oil and convinced OPEC to follow suit in an oil embargo. Overnight, the price of gas at the pump doubled and people had to wait in lines that extended for miles. King Faisal informed Henry Kissinger, the Secretary of State at the time, that he wanted to pray in Jerusalem's Al-Aqsa mosque during his lifetime. Shortly afterwards he was assassinated and the oil embargo fell apart. He never prayed in Jerusalem.

In 1972, President Richard Nixon's re-election campaign was bogged down by anti-war demonstrators who camped across the street from the White House at the mall. He went out one night and tried to convince the demonstrators of the legitimacy of his Vietnam War. They were not impressed. Still, he won the election but lost the White House and America lost the war.

They say that history keeps repeating itself or maybe it just rhymes bringing up the same unresolved issues over and over. President Bush went to Texas to enjoy himself and all of a sudden a grieving mother showed up outside his ranch. Cindy Sheehan lost her son in Iraq and a few months later separated from her husband. She intensified her anti-war activism and decided to camp outside the President's ranch. Then, the news cameras carried her story and other anti-war activists joined Cindy's camp.

Whenever the President left his ranch the story was more about Cindy than where the President was going. She put him under siege in his own ranch. He began defending his Iraq policy and addressing Cindy's comments directly. She managed to engage the President in a debate more heated than the Presidential debate with Senator John Kerry.

Major news organizations started using the phrase "the majority of Americans do not support the war in Iraq." Bush had lost the war.

In this day and age a war is a publicity campaign in the first vein. Bush has clearly lost the war for the hearts and minds of the American people. The only thing left for him is to withdraw from Iraq with some dignity. It is the same thing that Israel demanded when it decided to withdraw from Gaza. It is called the "Syria withdrawal syndrome." No one wants to catch it especially Israel and the United States. They put so much pressure on Syria this past spring till it ran out of Lebanon with its tail between its legs. Now, the Syrian regime is a sitting duck waiting to be pummeled by any bully. The political irony of things is that "what goes around comes around." Now it's their turn to cut and run with their tails between their legs. How many occupations will it take for bully nations to understand that the logic of occupation can NEVER work?

Skyrocketing gas prices, war in the Middle East and an economy running on empty. It sounds like 1973 all over. At this rate a scandal must break soon for the President which will lead him to resign in disgrace some time next year.

Christian extremist Pat Robertson declared that Venezuelan President Hugo Chavez must be assassinated by the United States. Chavez has been an international critic of the war in Iraq and has managed to hold on to his legitimate presidency despite a failed coup. He fell out of favor with America's foreign policy a few years back when he decided unilaterally to nationalize Venezuelan oil companies and declare them owned by the state. Big American oil companies lost big money in the one-sided deal. So, now we can conclude that God has promised America the oil of this world just like He promised the Jews the land of Palestine.

Just before the war in 2003 the price of a barrel of oil was under $30. We went to war to destroy Saddam's WMD's. But we could not find them. So then we declared that our war liberated the Iraqi people and we began peddling the idea of freedom and democracy in the Middle East. Then, Muslim extremists took over the process and stuck the Sharia law in the Iraqi constitution. O.k. so we lost the war for democracy and now we will settle for a theocracy similar to Iran's.

All the while most people believed that the war was waged in the name of oil and Haliburton. So where is the oil? Show me the oil. The sacrifices of our troops will not be wasted if we take over the Iraqi oil. Why did the price of oil climb to $65 per barrel?

Because of basic laws of supply and demand. Demand for oil began climbing at a very fast rate last year. The first sign came during the electric blackout of August 2003. We have not built a new nuclear power plant in over 25 years. The Chinese economy had been growing at a double digit rate for the past ten years. All of a sudden the Chinese people parked their bicycles and began buying cars. Southeast Asia demanded more oil and America loved its V8 gas guzzling monstrous SUV's. We had an energy policy focused on drilling new oil fields in the Alaskan wildlife preserves instead of encouraging car makers to speed up the production of electric cars.

In the roaring Nineties, we implemented environmental policies that allowed every state to legislate its own emissions standard. We ended up with over 50 gasoline standards thereby increasing processing cost and choking off overall refining capacity.

Now, America is in dire need of an energy policy that makes us less dependent on oil. A policy that encourages ingenuity in mass producing electric cars which deliver environmental cleanliness and new jobs for America.

September 3, 2005

Ignorance is NOT bliss

After a long discussion on the war on terror with a university graduate who works in the film industry, she turned to me and said: so you're telling me Arabs don't live in Afghanistan. I was taken aback at first and then realized that she had very little knowledge about the world outside of her own sphere. I answered with strained patience: No

Arabs do not live or inhabit Afghanistan. It is inhabited by another type of people who speak a different language and come from Asian tribal ancestry.

It is a shame but ignorance rules in society. A recent survey showed that only 17 percent of the people could point out the location of Afghanistan on a map. My friend continued "so we went to war right after September 11th with people that were not even Arab?" I said: that's correct. She snapped indignantly "I knew it. I knew George Bush lied to us." At this point I could no longer sustain the conversation. Imam Ali, May God bless his soul, the Prophet Muhammad's cousin, had a famous saying; "I never met a learned man that I could not defeat in debate but never have I defeated an ignorant man."

One can not reason with ignorance. It is based on stubborn insistence that lack of information is good. The inability to absorb information, store it in the memory and later connect it with other related information causes a society to behave like it has Alzheimer's disease.

I spent six hours one day with an out of state journalist who was doing a story on Arab Americans in Dearborn. I told him that "Dearborn has the largest concentration of Arabs outside of the Middle East." It is a famous line used by many of us to describe the uniqueness of our beloved city. Prior experience with journalists dictated that I repeated what I had said many times. So every now and then I made sure I repeated that same line. I took him to an Arabic restaurant and inducted him into eating Kibbe Niyyi which is truly authentic Lebanese food. I always try to culturize people who come to visit Dearborn because I believe that in the end that's all they ever remember of their visit. I don't rely much on their information retention rate.

So I repeated our famous line about Arabs in Dearborn at least six times. The paper came out a few days later and the article read "Dearborn, Michigan, is the largest Arab city in the world outside the Middle East." I laughed. That's all I could do. One can not make war with ignorance. We just have to keep repeating our lines over and over like parrots till it sinks in.

The media is the mirror of a society. I don't fault journalists for not absorbing much information but when they have a tape recorder and they write everything one tells them, and still make critical errors then the entire industry is suffering from a chronic disease of ignorance. Whatever is written by a journalist is usually checked by an editor

98

before it is printed. How can this editor print a sentence saying that Dearborn is the largest Arab city outside of the Middle East. Dearborn is in America. How could it be an Arab city if it is in America! I go back to what I said earlier about reason and common sense. The media is no longer interested in talking about reasons why things happen. They hardly cover any causes of events. They had become so addicted to action just like our film industry. They want to talk about the act itself but never about what caused it.

We turn on the local nightly news and the same thing seems to happen every night. They report the same action while substituting different names. We hear this every day: "…was shot and killed but the police has no motive…bank was robbed and the neighborhood was terrified…arrested and charged with domestic violence…etc…" The same approach has also extended to foreign policy. "…died due to a bomb blast in Baghdad…suspected terrorists were shot at a military checkpoint…etc…"

The American media industry is the richest and most resourceful media in the world. Most news reporters truly believe in the message of journalism. They carry a heavy responsibility but they can't help being an empty shell. The industry has become so commercialized and needy of following breaking stories that it had turned good journalism into a machine that churns out the same information every where you look.

They are all running after the same story and it gets reported on all channels and even at the same time. The media moguls truly believe that the American people are a blank sheet of paper and they become according to what you tell them. They perpetuate ignorance by reporting the most minimum while giving people the impression that they have reported everything that is out there.

The print media is run by straight-jacketed corporate conservatives that deceive themselves into thinking that their articles are gospel. They truly believe that their stories can not be faulted. The New York Times believes that it is the conscience of America. CNN considers itself the standard of impartiality while Fox News acts as if it is running the country.

It is true that public opinion is shaped by the information out there. But there is a constant power struggle between politicians and the media to shape that public opinion.

In 1960 the movie "Lawrence of Arabia" shattered all records of success and made Arab actor Omar Sharif a household name. Most people believe that it is a real depiction of Arabs and their culture. Well, it showed that most Arabs were hungry bedouins thirsting for blood. It showed their leaders as indecisive pensive opportunists with repressed homosexual desires. The whole Arab world in the movie was always a desert or a barren rocky land. I enjoyed it as much as the next person but I never got my education from a movie like that.

Education is the foundation of our civilized society. The media reflects the level of collective education that a society attains to. American society is still one of the most educated in the world. That's why the media industry here is so colossal and fortunate with vast resources. American society believes in the media.

Our Arab community has little belief in the power of the media to shape our lives. That's why the Arab American media is somewhat malnourished, underdeveloped and always struggling to stay afloat. Unless we begin to feed it, our message will go no where.

September 10, 2005

Why is Education Important?

When I was in fourth grade I had a history teacher who told us interesting stories. He spoke of the human spirit and great tragedies of war. He narrated personal stories of Kings who had dreams for their people. He personalized the stories of great people who strived to create a human society built on ideals. He told us of the glory of great cultures and how civilizations were built by immense sacrifice and unshakeable faith in ideas. I loved his stories as the historical characters came to life in my imagination and I was transformed into another world. I felt the pain of these historical figures and my heart danced with joy when they were triumphant.

I grew up believing that history was current and live. It was not something that happened in the distant past and had no relevance to our lives. Till today I find myself reading history books with incredible interest. Whenever I pick up one of these books I fall into the old familiar intoxicating trance. That teacher had an incredible effect on my life. He was able to get me hooked so to speak and I have been happily addicted to the subject of history for over three decades now.

100

My early years in school as a child inspired me to greater things in life and gave me dreams to live for. The character of my teachers in those formative years molded the shape of my world. I looked up to some of them as role models and mimicked those whom I admired the most. They did not need to teach me values because I absorbed their values, and I tried to behave the way they behaved. For the most part, they were kind, gentle, considerate, humble, patient, genuine, honest and caring people. I grew up with those values implanted deep in my heart.

We can not underestimate the profound effect that our teachers have on kids. They hold the power to make them love or hate education.

Our state of education on a national level has been steadily declining. That's because society has been moving at a faster pace in terms of technology. The educational institutions with their incredibly bureaucratic machines have been too slow to adapt. They will always be playing catch-up and that's the nature of the game. However, they need to speed up the pace of their catch-up in order to stay relevant.

We send our kids to high schools and unfortunately all they learn is how to be cool. I talk to kids every day. They have enormous energies that go un-channeled. They are not challenged enough. They have constant "issues" with their teachers and their teachers have "issues" with them. There is a break-down of communications between the two parties and there is little feedback. It is unclear who the customer is in this system.

But it is very clear in my mind. Students are the customers. They need to be taught useful skills, ethics and values. They need to be prepared for the jobs of the 21st century. We can not continue feeding them useless information and pretend that the university will clean up the mess. Most will never make it that far. We need to raise the standard of education. We need to raise the bar of our expectations and ask for more.

I have a deep belief in the message of education. It is the foundation of our human civilization. That's why I decided to run for a seat on the School Board in Dearborn. My name will be on the ballot in the upcoming election on November 8th. There are four candidates running for two open seats. I kindly ask for your vote.

September 17, 2005

Who is to blame for Hurricane Katrina?

Human misery anywhere leads to misery everywhere. That is a fact we must accept.

As we watched hurricane Katrina pulverize the coastal line of three states extending the vast ocean into earthly plains, it was like a scene from a science-fiction movie. Fish swam in the streets of New Orleans and homes became spawning grounds for shrimp and crab. It was the worst natural disaster ever recorded in the history of the United States.

Natural disasters bring out the best and worst in humanity. On the downside, opportunity opened up for looters and thieves. They have a way of surviving natural disasters like cock roaches that can survive a nuclear holocaust. They are usually strong-willed young men who can easily swim or climb to the rooftops of buildings. The torrent of the flood engulfs those who seek the least risk in life. The weak in society usually die first like the elderly and children who trapped themselves in the false security of locked up bunkers and basement shelters.

And like cock roaches the thieves spread in the city of New Orleans busting into stores and stealing any thing of value. The word got out and thieves from the tri-state area converged on the city of Big Easy. They came in boats, trucks and some stole buses to get there. It was a feeding frenzy and it reminded me of scenes from Baghdad right after the liberation. Gangs of young men piled up goods on trucks or carried TV's or pieces of furniture, and smiled to the cameras. But there were also smart and organized thieves who did not waste their time with such bulky stuff that is worth so little. They hit the jewelry stores, banks and high tech. They stole the smallest items that weighed the least and yielded the highest returns.

In the absence of law enforcement or the military the streets were patrolled by armed gangs who took control of enclaves. Some policemen were killed execution-style as they tried to hide from the people whom they had tormented the most. It was a policeman's worst nightmare as the order of society flipped overnight and he became the hunted.

Lawlessness, disorder, starvation, people with bullet holes in their head, naked babies, scared mothers, hungry children. It was like all the disasters that we see on television from all regions of the world had

102

come together in New Orleans. The social order broke down and the result was appalling. Morality, ethics and brotherly love did not rise to the top. The master of the scene was chaos, anarchy and greed.

I have always said that America is an economy. People in America only tolerate each other so they can make money off of each other. They are held back from killing each other by the brute force of police. Remove the police and observe if the people would police themselves. That's the real test of a society that believes in the institution of human justice.

Our society failed that test miserably in New Orleans. We had to send in the national guards and troops came in armored tanks and fought battles to regain control of the city. It was a military operation similar to the invasion of any Iraqi city.

Our commander-in-chief, President Bush, rode in the liberated streets this week in a military convoy and inspected the destruction. I have always advocated for the invasion and liberation of most inner cities of America. We don't need to look too far for military adventures and invasion opportunities. I think our President will begin to see that invading foreign lands is not as critical as the need to invade let's say Detroit and clean it up.

Natural disasters bring out the best and worst in humanity. On the upside, America came together in a remarkable outpouring of charity and generosity. The entire nation became united like never before in helping the victims and the homeless. It was a rare type of unity founded on the most noble of sentiments; helping a fellow man out of his misery.

There is a passage in the Qur'an which I read all the time to remind myself of God's absolute awesome power over our lives.

"We will send upon you disasters that will put your faith to the test.
Periods of fear, times of hunger, lack of money and loss of life.
And your labors will fruition to nothing,
but the good news will come to those who persevere.
They are the people when hit by a disaster who say:
we are one with God and He will always be our destination.
 They are the ones who have a connection with their Lord,
and He watches over them with compassion as they proceed on a gifted path."
(Al-Baqara (the Cow) verses 155-157)

Who can we blame or hate for hurricane Katrina? There is no one to blame or to direct anger towards. We can not hate the very nature that we came from. The forces of death always intertwine with the forces of life. But hope springs eternal from the human spirit.

The only thing we can do is to be prepared for the disasters that God will bring upon us to test our faith. Have we brought hurricane Katrina upon ourselves? Have we become so corrupt of a society that God's intervention has become necessary to save us? Or things like that just happen for no reason and all this talk of God is for the weak and superstitious?

I don't believe that anything that happens in nature is unrelated to the behavior of man. We exist as part of a natural cosmic order. If we abuse that order it abuses us back. If we become so abusive of each other something bigger than all of us happens as a direct result of our collective actions. Whether you believe in God, nature, Buddha, Zen, Jehova, Jesus, Allah, science, atheism, secularism or whatever. It doesn't really matter because it all boils down to one thing: expect the consequences of every action you take to reflect directly upon your life. You will be treated like you treat others.

Do the poor people of Louisiana, Mississippi and Alabama deserve the wrath of God? No, they certainly do not. No one deserves misery and no misery should be wished upon any people. Because misery anywhere is misery everywhere. It is only a matter of time for misery inflicted upon others to catch up with the tyrants who perpetuate it.

Our response to Katrina: we need to practice more goodness and seek forgiveness in the course of every action we take.

September 24, 2005

The false promise of Insurance

Over 17 years ago and after volunteering for three months to work for free on the (1988) Jesse Jackson for President Campaign I found myself penniless and in danger of being evicted from my small apartment in a town north of Pittsburgh. An insurance salesman knocked on my door while I was writing a book.

The salesman began his pitch as soon as I said hello. Then, he pushed his way into my living room and sat comfortably on a couch while I was still standing debating whether to let him in. He had a deep warm southern accent that stretched every word as if it sprang from the bottom of his heart. He was sincere, genuine and engaging. I admired his people skill and wished I had some of that.

Then, I steered the conversation away from insurance to politics. He listened intently as I spoke connecting one issue to the next and making a full diagnosis of society's ailments.

After an hour or so he asked if I would be interested in becoming an insurance salesman. Being penniless and writing a hopeless book I asked about the pay. He said it was all commission-based and I could write my own paycheck. The sky was the limit and I could make as much money as I wanted. I was never afraid of hard work and so I gave it a try.

The following week the company sent me to Philadelphia for a 3-day crash course to prepare for the state licensing exam. I was enthusiastic and I applied myself studying almost 18 hours a day. On the fifth day I took the exam and when the results came out I had scored third in the entire state. The general manager pegged me as a rising star and came to my hotel room to chart my career path.

I spent the following week in sales school learning the scripted pitch by heart and memorizing lines to rebut every objection that a customer may conceivably have. The policy that they trained me to sell was called "Accidental Death and Dismemberment Insurance Policy". It paid money directly to the beneficiary in case of death or dismemberment as a result of an accident. Our commission was 40 percent of the policy price. We practiced till I was singing the lines in my sleep.

They gave me a territory and they set me loose. I hit the trailer parks and far out villages where people worked in coal mines or on farms. I walked the streets going from door to door and never letting a slammed door stand in my way of having a positive attitude when I knocked on the following door. I walked in the snow. I stood in the rain. I fought with ferocious dogs and wrestled with drunken men. I was determined to succeed and I did. My best customers were the poorest people on this earth who could not afford to bury their loved ones. They believed in the piece of paper that I was selling. The more policies I sold the less I believed in the promise of insurance.

People believed in insurance as a form of salvation and I began to detest the papers I peddled. I quit six months later because I found myself trying to convince a customer that insurance was part of the systemized falsehood that we have imbued in our society. Our security safety net has become the insurance company and the welfare system. Where is God, family and community in this equation? I guess people had lost faith in them.

We are required by law to carry car insurance. People in Detroit and many zip codes in Dearborn have been red lined as very high risk. No-fault insurance for a middle-aged person in these areas costs almost $2,500 per year. Most of the cars insured are not worth that much.

Before September 11th I used to pay $600 per year for my homeowners insurance. Now, I pay $1,800 and when I asked why they said: because of September 11th. Now, hurricane Katrina will do wonders to our insurance premiums as if we'd been hit by the storm. Many insurance companies will declare bankruptcy and that may not be a bad thing. Falsehood has to fall somehow and God is sending Rita after Katrina, maybe to tell us that our trust is misplaced.

For many years my employers paid for my health insurance. Then, a few years ago I began paying the premium. The rates kept creeping up. Then, one day I decided to cancel it and to put my faith in God. I overcame my fear of the unknown and my fear of going bankrupt if my health went bad. Most of all, I liberated myself from the idea that insurance was a guarantee of life. God only guarantees life and He takes what He gives.

The insurance industry in America is almost 15% of our economy. It owns the prime real estate and the towering buildings in most of our cities. They push paper all day long and send lawyers to negotiate with other lawyers who represent victims. Somebody walks in front of my house on what is called "my" sidewalk. He slips and falls. Then, he files a lawsuit asking for thousands in damages.

I turn it over to my insurance company and they settle the case preferring not to go to court. Most insurance companies do not favor litigation as it places their destiny in the hands of a jury. Juries are known to be "victim-biased".

Personal injury law is destroying our system of democracy. It is unconstitutional because it assigns unequal value to human suffering.

106

A broken arm in Detroit is not worth the same as a broken arm in Bloomfield Hills. In any case, most of the money is taken by lawyers. On average, the victim ends up with no more than 30% of the settlement money.

Lawyers are ruling society because people are sold on the idea of suing each other. It has turned an honorable profession into a parasitic activity.

We need to cap the value of each injury and create a uniform guideline for compensation. For example, a broken arm would receive $2,000 whether it's in Beverly Hills or in Chicago.

Liability law is important in holding people responsible, when they are found negligent of their duties towards others. But the system has gone mad and society is paying for it. We are all being punished instead of negligent individuals. It is time for lawmakers to fix this problem before it breaks our backs.

October 1, 2005

Ramadan: Time to Fast and Reflect

In a few short days the month of Ramadan will start and observing Muslims all around the world will begin their fast, from dawn till dusk. On this occasion I wish every person a month full of God's blessings (Ramadan Mubarak).

The story of the messenger of Islam, the Prophet Muhammad Bin Abdallah Bin Abd Al-Muttalib of the Hashemite tribe, may God's most blessings of peace be showered upon him, began exactly 1436 years ago. He was forty years old and used to retreat to a cave in the rocky mountains overlooking his home in Mecca. The cave, called Hira'a, provided seclusion and solitude to reflect in God's creation. One day, while he was in the cave an angel appeared to him and told him to read. He answered inquisitively "read what". The angel shook him and asked him to read again. The messenger answered again "read what". The angel, known as Gabriel, did the same thing for a third time and got the same answer from the prophet.

That's when Gabriel began reciting:
(1) Read in the Name of the Lord your God the Creator,
(2) who created man out of a clinging clot.

107

(3) Read by the Grace of the Lord your God the Most Benign,
(4) who taught man by the use of the pen,
(5) that which man did not know.

And it was the beginning of the revelation of the holy book Al-Qur'an, which literally means the "Reading". Ramadan is the month that commemorates the opening of the portal of inspiration and the beginning of the revered revelations to the messenger of Islam. The book and its teachings have inspired hundreds of millions throughout the ages. It reshaped the human civilization and created a culture rich with human values.

The word in the Qur'an spread like wild fire because it appealed to the common man and gave him hope that he was equal to the rich and powerful. It turned slaves into free men and gave dignity and respect to women. It created a law reflecting man's instinctual oneness with nature and his universe.

It is untrue that the prophet Muhammad was illiterate as it is untrue that Islam spread by the power of the sword. The prophet was an institution of knowledge and a beacon of enlightenment. He was a well-rounded and balanced man in all aspects. He had traveled extensively in his younger days and had become intimately familiar with the ideologies that preceded his day, and the political structures that ruled his world.

He was the only prophet from the line of the Patriarch Abraham who was able to develop a complete theology, teach it to his people, transform their culture and then create a system of government, all within his lifetime. No other prophet including Abraham, Moses, and Jesus was able to achieve such an accomplishment. He was the fulfillment of all their dreams, hopes and inspirations. That's why he was the final messenger. The words uttered by his own lips are contained in the Qur'an. But not every word he ever said is in the Qur'an. Only the holy inspiration coming directly from God (through the angel Gabriel), or as it is called in Arabic "Wahi".

Every Ramadan I read the Qur'an from beginning to end and I marvel at the layers of meanings contained in the symphonic-style that weaves words into sentences that rhyme. The language lends itself to easy recitation as it rings echoes of meanings. That is the miracle of the Qur'an in Arabic.

If you are interested in learning more about the life of Muhammad I recommend the following book in English: Muhammad, his life based on the earliest sources, written by Martin Lings.

Fasting in this holy month brings spiritual and health benefits. It equalizes the poor with the rich in the indiscriminate feeling of hunger and thirst. It breaks down barriers between people and joins them in their common humanity.

The following are some verses from the Qur'an concerning Ramadan:

(183) O people of faith: you have been commanded to fast.
The same way others before you have been commanded.
In this way, you may learn to fear the consequences of wrongdoing.

(184) For a limited number of days set in a calendar.
But if one of you is sick or traveling then he is exempt.
You may make up the lost days by fasting some other days.
For some people it is beyond their power to fast,
they are to feed a poverty-stricken person instead.
This is a voluntary act of goodness,
and the benefit is directly reflected upon the volunteer.
But if you try your best to fast that is good for you,
as long as you are willing to learn.

(185) It was in the month of Ramadan that the Qur'an was revealed,
as a guide for mankind with self-evident truths to discern falsehood.
If Ramadan arrives and you happen to be at one location then you are to fast.
But if you happen to be sick or in transit then you may eat on those certain days, provided that they are made up at a later time.
God wants you to fulfill your obligations with ease and not through undue hardship, and to complete your fast.
The purpose is to expand God's role in the enlightenment of humanity, and to become eternally grateful.

(186) If My servants ask about Me.
Tell them: I am very close to them and I respond to their prayer when they call onto Me.
Tell them: listen to Me and believe in Me,
so you may attain to maturity of faith.

(187) You have been sanctioned to join with your women at night during the days of the fast.

They protect you from the nakedness of instinctual need as you protect them just like garments do, each covering the need of the other.
God knows that you have been joining with women at night and feeling guilty about it.
He has forgiven you and accepted your penance.
Now, you may go to them and satisfy your desire the way God has permitted.
Eat and drink till the crack of dawn when you can distinguish a white thread from a black one.
Then, make your fast until nightfall.
Do not couple with your wives in places of worship.
These are God's precincts and should not be violated.
Thus, God clarifies His significations to people,
so they may avoid error and sin.
Surah Al-Baqara (Chapter2- The Cow, Verses 183-187)

October 8, 2005

Empowerment

I need your attention for just one second please. Elections take place every year. It is fixed in the constitution that elections are to be held on the first Tuesday of November. This year, the elections are scheduled for Tuesday, November 8, 2005. Please go out and vote. It only takes a few minutes of your time but the return on this investment is tremendous.

Some of us take many things for granted and assume that most people know what we know. Especially when it comes to politics and how the system works. Most people are not familiar with the mechanics and the procedures of the system, which leads them to stay away.

Voting is a right that guarantees your existence. In the eyes of the system you do not exist unless you vote. Born as a stateless Palestinian I have been campaigning most of my life to get the attention of others and to let them know that I do exist.

When I first arrived in this country almost 27 years ago people were calling me all kinds of names thinking that I was from Iran. Back then, the hostage crisis with Iran was dominating the news. When I explained to them that I was not from Iran and that I was an Arab they showed some understanding. But Americans are not ethnocentric and I found that when one displays too much pride in his ethnicity he gets

110

penalized for it. America is built on melting people's ethnicity and remolding them in a common human culture. It is the melting pot.

Recently, I put my name on the ballot in Dearborn and am running for a seat on its school board. It has been a wonderful experience so far. Most of the people I meet on the campaign trail are very kind and sincere. They care about the quality of education and they follow the news of the school system.

Americans of Arabic descent are almost one third of the population in Dearborn but their kids make up 50 percent of the student population. The 7-member school board does not reflect this diversity. In fact, there is not a single member on the board who is Arabic. This creates problems of cultural misunderstanding and an inability to cater to the development needs of almost half of the student population. It is a classic example of under representation.

Our schools are like our democracy. They are by the people and for the people. Now, what does a school board do? They oversee and manage all the operations of the schools. They are responsible for making all the policies that deliver education in the city. You can think of them as if they are the US Congress but just for the schools in our city. They hold the executive branch (the Superintendent and his administrative team) accountable for implementing their policies and following their decisions.

Does a school board member get involved in disputes and complaints made by students or parents? Of course they do, because they are elected by the people to represent their interest. So, the board member is accountable to all the citizens of Dearborn.

All members of the board are honorable people. It is a thankless job that deals with issues that are very personal to people. When a kid is sent home from school it is very personal. When a kid comes home crying from school it is very personal. When a kid is flunking it is very personal.

The job of the member of the board is not political in nature, like the post of a State Representative for example. It hardly pays any money but deals with the most intense sentiments. Like, earlier this year there was a teacher who said some disrespectful words about the Qur'an in his classroom. Over a hundred members of the Muslim community in Dearborn went to the board and urged board members to fire the teacher. The teacher was suspended from his post and transferred to another location. But he was never fired.

Now, if there was one Muslim member on the board the situation would have been handled in a much cooler and calmer fashion. Members of the Muslim community felt that they had to educate the board about their religion and the significance of their holy book. Most felt that the board did not even understand the basics of their culture and faith.

The result of that episode is that it became glaringly obvious that 50 percent of the student population and their parents were not adequately represented on the board. This hurt the unity of our city and threatened the good relations that we had worked so hard to build between the two communities. The board desperately needs the active engagement of an Arab Muslim in its policy-making proceedings.

The great majority of the citizens of Dearborn want to see an Arab American elected to the board not because of his ethnicity but because they care about the unity of Dearborn. They want to see a strong candidate who will not shy away from addressing the hard issues. They want to see a board member who has the calmness and the common sense to break down barriers of ignorance and join all Dearbornites in their common humanity.

Politics is about differences and a grab for power. Education is about breaking down differences and removing barriers between people that were erected on the foundation of ignorance. There is no room for politics in the education of children. Politics should not enter into the race for the Dearborn board of education. I will not allow anyone to say anything negative about any of the four candidates. They are all honorable people who put their talents in the service of their community.

My message to everyone is one of participation and empowerment. Our greatest challenge is getting people's attention and informing them that there is an election on November 8. This is going to be an exceptionally low turnout election and so every single vote is going to make a difference. So, please go to the polls and tell the world that you do exist.

October 15, 2005

My Life

My father who is now in the heavens used to tell me when I was younger "if God loves you He'll show His creation." What he meant was that in some mysterious way God will take me all over the globe and open my eyes and heart to the full depth of the human experience.

I've had a blessed life. I can't complain. And God has shown me the wonders of His creation. I have lived in Europe, worked in Alaska and lounged on white sand beaches in Florida. But most of all I have seen the human spirit and experienced the pain of being human. I have collected memories and stories that can last a lifetime to write about.

One day I will have a grandchild and I will tell him this story. I am not married now but I've had two short-lived failed marriages in the past. I am blessed with enormous love from my family and friends. These are people who stood by me in good times and bad times. They have been at my side like a brick wall. They never wavered once in offering their generous love and support. That's the circle of people that I treasure so deeply in my heart. They are with me wherever I go and some day I hope to stand before God and testify about the goodness that these people have shown me, and I pray in some small way I will help them get to heaven.

I came to this country in 1979 to go to the university. I got my bachelors' degree in Civil Engineering and went on to get my Masters degree in Engineering Management. I finished from the university in 1986 but I had already been working since the first day I landed in this great country. I started out cleaning tables at the cafeteria in the university, then became a dish washer, then drove a taxi and then began working in the corporate world in 1982.

I was never afraid of hard work and was never ashamed of any type of work. I worked in oil refineries and then became a construction manager overseeing interior renovations of high rise buildings in downtown Philadelphia. Then, I went on to become a business management consultant. That's when I began living out of a suitcase and a hotel room.

I criss-crossed the nation going to wherever work took me. I had projects in every type of industry from car plants to bakeries to soft drink bottling companies to food distribution, just to name a few.

113

Meanwhile, my permanent address had become in Dearborn, Michigan as most of my family had moved here after my father's death.

Then, I got involved heavily in social issues and became very active in our community. I supported all their good causes and articulated their sentiments in interviews, papers and in most legislative and media outlets. I also started business concerns in Detroit. One of them was a car dealership.

Right after September 11, 2001, I had some complaints from customers. I resolved the complaints but some members of the Detroit police department had gotten involved. Then, a few months later in 2002, I was charged with a criminal complaint.

It was one of the hardest ordeals that I had to face in my life. It ranked up there with the other trials and tribulations of my life. The charges were aired all over the local TV stations and in the newspapers. I did not hide or run away. I faced them and went to one court hearing after the other for 22 months. Then, I became broke from the legal fees and my lawyer advised me to accept a plea agreement that was offered.

I pleaded no contest to some charges and was sentenced to five years probation. I ended up with a criminal record

I am now running for a seat on the board of education in Dearborn. I have had a great experience so far campaigning for the betterment of our schools.

The local newspapers are running articles about me saying that I have a criminal record. I tell everyone that I am human and I have made a mistake in the past and I paid dearly for it. And I have become a better man throughout this experience. My heart has been expanded with a greater capacity for forgiveness, tolerance, and sympathy for the plight of others. My brother will attest to that. He's seen my transformation and he tells me that I have finally matured.

I had a dream earlier this year. I was in a dark dungeon. There was a tunnel ahead and a bright light at the end. I was trapped with two huge snakes. As I was suffocating in my dream I gathered all my courage and wrestled with one of the snakes and killed it. All of a sudden the door opened up and I ran through the tunnel. I came into blinding sunlight and found myself in a gladiators' arena. It was just like the movie. I was in the middle of a Roman stage with a sword in my hand

114

expected to fight for my life. The crowds began cheering and I looked at them bewildered. Then, I woke up.

Now, I know what the dream means. The arena is elections and the candidates are the gladiators. They must kill each other in order to please the cheering crowds. There was only one man who was able to unite the gladiators and stop them from killing each other. He led a revolt against Caesar and almost succeeded. His name was Spartacus and his story lives through the movie that was made by Kirk Douglas in 1960.

Whenever I watch that movie I feel a lump in my throat and I choke up from the tyranny that powerful men cause unto lesser men.

November 5, 2005

Participation

Please go out and vote on Tuesday, November 8. Participation is the fiber of existence. It is the essence of society and our human civilization. We are participants in everything that takes place in the corridor of life, whether we like it or not.

The spirit of the collective lives through participation. Communication is the tool of participation. We are all connected through one essence that runs through the tangible material of the universe. Everyone and everything in this universe communicate with each other and depend on each other. The tree sways when the wind blows. This is a form of communication.

As human beings we've been looking for a way to communicate to each other our collective will since we emerged from the cave. The Greeks came up with the idea of democracy or rule by the people and for the people. Then, we had thousands of years of ideological inventions or religious thoughts injected into it. Now, we are struggling as a human civilization to combine both and come up with an ethical and moral rule of the people and by the people.

Our laws and the way we govern depend very much on the people we elect as our representatives. They say that the best customer is an educated customer and the best voter is the one who had done his/her homework. Elections come around every year for a different set of offices and this year it is all about local issues.

115

This is not a presidential race or even a mid term election but it is important because it determines the way this city will be governed. Literature has been published every where about the candidates and what they will do if they are elected. This is your time to communicate your wishes and to hire new representatives or fire some.

In our political structure decisions are made by those who participate. Our community has the numbers to sway most local elections and to cast the deciding vote. But we need to go out and vote. It only takes a few minutes of our busy day but it makes a great difference to everyone. We have issues that we have been fighting for years, and if we don't elect those who stand with us we will not make any progress.

Do you want soccer fields in a park? Do you want respect for your culture and religion? Do you want to protect freedom and civil liberties? Do you want to be part of the decision-making or do you want others to make decisions for you?

All these are questions you can only answer by showing up at the poll and casting your ballot. Most churches in America were used as the pulpit to elect George Bush yet our mosques still shy away from politics. Our people don't get enough political awareness education at mosques and so they stay away. It is natural for a human being not to participate in something he does not understand.

Well, it is very simple; you stand to lose a lot by not participating in the political process. Let me put it this way; you stand to lose your very existence in America. As Arab Americans, we have been under the microscope of suspicion since 9/11 and it is no coincidence that they are building one of the largest FBI centers in the nation right here in Detroit.

Islam is a complete religion with social, economic and political facets. We need a religious fatwa (edict) by all Muslim Imams that makes voting "halal". If you ask any Imam of any mosque how many registered voters do you have in your congregation? He'll say: thousands. But really they don't know the numbers, because they have not paid attention to the business of politics in this country. It is not about fiery sermons and passionate pleas. It is all about turning your vote out for a certain candidate on Election Day. Everything else does not make any difference.

We have large voting blocks in our highly attended mosques waiting to be harnessed in the service of our issues. All we need is strong leadership from the religious community to deliver the vote. Our system depends and thrives on participation.

In the political equation we do not count unless we stand at the poll and tell people that we care about our issues, and that we care about our way of life. If we don't do that others will make decisions on our behalf and in default. Then, we can not complain, and we can't say that we did not have a chance to express ourselves.

We don't get too many chances to express our dissatisfaction or satisfaction with the way things are going. These are decisive moments where we can fire an official and hire a new one. If you don't want to make that decision somebody else will do it for you. Then, you can not blame them for the policies they will be passing, and you can not blame them for telling you how to live and how to behave in society. You never communicated what you wanted, and therefore they will only listen to those who vote.

The choice is yours. Do you want to be the master of your destiny or are you happy following the orders of others who really don't care about you or your people. It is that simple.

November 12, 2005

Lessons from a local election

A friend of mine whom I went to school with 25 years ago called me from New Jersey last week. He said: you are a brave man to be running for public office. He added that my chances of winning were slim to none. I agreed. But he also said something that I refuse to believe. He said that as long as your God is not my God we will never trust you.

I told him that my God was the same God as his. He disagreed. I told him that we were all God's children. He disagreed again. He then made a matter-of-fact statement: if you do not accept Jesus Christ as your personal savior you will never be electable in this country. I told him that politics had more gray areas than his black and white ideas. He was sympathetic but stressed that he attended church every week and he knew the political messages coming out of the pulpit.

I looked at the results of my election. My hypothesis is that politics is like marketing a new name. If you have name recognition you will get elected. Nothing else matters. It really has nothing to do with religion or ethnic issues. The name "Canon" is a household name and therefore very electable. My name, on the other hand, is unknown and needs wide marketing. Citywide, I got almost 5 percent of the total vote and in East Dearborn where there is a higher percentage of Arab Americans I got 20 percent of the vote.

I came fourth in a field of four because my name had the least exposure. One of the candidates is an incumbent and her name had appeared at least four times on the ballot. The other two had run last year and came close to winning. So, my name had the least ballot exposure and that's why it finished last.

I estimate the total number of Arab votes that I had received around 400 out of the 1,435 votes. So, in the end I received a higher number of votes from non-Arab voters than from Arab voters. Thus, my friend's theory has no validity.

Elections are a game of numbers. It's all about getting people out to the polls to vote. It is also about mobilizing strong reputable people to lobby at the polls on Election Day. I had an aggressive elderly campaigner stand at a West end precinct all day for me, and the numbers from that poll station were double the average per location.

But let's look at the bigger picture. Most East end precincts where there is a concentration of Arab Americans had a turn out of about 18 percent. Precinct 15- Woodworth School had a sad turnout of 13 %, and only 141 voters showed up out of 1,110 registered. At the other end of town; the West end where the majority of voters are non-Arab the average turnout was in the mid thirties, almost double the rate of Arab voters. At precinct 32-Bryant Branch Library, the turnout was a whopping 37 % and 388 voters cast a ballot out of 1,056 registered. Overall, voter turnout was higher than anticipated coming at 31% in all of Dearborn.

Elections are a game of numbers and maybe that is something that our Arab American voter does not understand. I estimate that we had at best about 2,000 Arab Americans participate in this election. That is very sad when we know that Arab Americans make up at least one third of the population of this city. 2,000 Arab Americans cast a ballot out of 17,749 which comes up to about 11 percent of the total vote. This is a classic case of under representation.

118

But maybe that's what our people want. Maybe they don't want to be part of a democracy. These are questions that need to be answered if they want to be part of the decision-making process. During the past holy month of Ramadan the mosques in Dearborn served more than 50,000 believers. In just one mosque on Tireman Street almost 8,000 people showed up for the Eid prayers. I am beginning to think that Arabs want a theocracy and not a democracy. How can we say that we want democracy in the Middle East when we don't participate in the democracy we live in!

I, personally, put an election flyer on more than 800 cars the first day of Eid. I shook the hands of more than a hundred people. If I had invested the same amount of energy at any church I am sure that I would have reaped much better results.

A candidate runs to win. But when I threw my hat in the ring I was under no illusion that I had the slightest chance of winning. I ran as "proof of existence" because the alternative was even more abysmal.

Most people told me Americans will never vote for an Arab so you better focus all your energy on your base. In the past three weeks that's all I did. But I found myself preaching the message of empowerment and arguing why people should even participate. I found that the level of political awareness in our community was so low. Our mosques hardly engage in educating our people how to protect their rights in a democracy, and they focus most of their energy on subjects that deal with heaven and hell and the hereafter.

The Arab American Political Action Committee (AAPAC) sent out thousands of flyers and organized a get-out-the-vote campaign to mobilize the Arab vote. The only thing it did not do is go into people's living rooms and lift them off the couch to go to the polls. The response from our people was very disappointing. The response was a slap in the face of candidates telling them that they did not need to champion these causes.

If I ever run for public office again, I think I will have to ignore the Arab American community in order to increase my chances of winning. I will have to invest my energy in places that have a higher level of political awareness.

On the upside we had a record number of Arab names appearing on the ballot. 12 out of 61 names were Arabic (20%). But because very few

Arabs went out to vote we only had 3 Arab names elected out of 20 winners (15%).

In the final analysis, we got 15 percent of the total public representation which is almost in line with the 11 percent rate of Arab American participation. In a democracy, proportionate representation always wins in the end.

November 26, 2005

Criminal records dog people for life

A couple of weeks ago the Supreme Court refused to hear an important case. Thirteen states have laws barring people with felony criminal records from voting. These states, mostly Republican controlled, have legislated that anyone with a felony record is barred from participating in elections or running for public office. In essence, they have taken away the rights of citizenship of anyone who gets a criminal record.

A California man got national attention earlier this month when he was elected to a school board while serving time in jail. He was an incumbent with a felony conviction and under probation. He violated the conditions of his probation two weeks before elections, and it landed him in jail. The matter was referred to the California legislature for legal advice regarding his re-election status.

It is estimated that almost 20 percent of the adult black male population has a felony record. The United States warehouses more than 3 million inmates in its prison system and graduates almost 600,000 a year. In his state of the union earlier this year, President Bush addressed this issue with a proposal to fund their re-entry into society.

Pressure on the justice system has been mounting for years. Twenty years ago the percentage of the population with a criminal record was much lower than it is today. In the nineties President Clinton passed the "Three Strikes Out" federal mandate in sentencing drug related offenses. It is commonly known in the justice community that the same offenders keep revolving in and out of the system. Thus, Clinton's intentions were honorable in keeping some of these offenders off the streets for good.

The "Three Strikes Out" mandate required judges to hand out life sentences to mostly drug dealers that are beyond rehabilitation. Shortly

120

thereafter the prisons began filling up to capacity. More prisons were built, more guards were hired and more taxes were levied. As Republicans swept through the political landscape of America more severe laws were passed and tougher judges were appointed to the bench.

The result is a criminal justice system busting at the seam and millions of people in society with criminal records. After 9/11 huge amounts of resources went into Homeland Security funding system upgrades and information accessibility. A person convicted of a felony twenty years ago would not have a record of that in the system. But a person convicted of a misdemeanor in the last 4 years would have his record plastered all over the place and within easy access by anyone.

The White House recognizes the dilemma between national security, access to individual records and the social dimension of this difficult issue. It advocates for monetary aid to people graduating from prison while its policies support isolating them from society. Like most of the Bush doctrine; it may sound good at the top but when it gets to the ground level it turns out to be the exact opposite thing.

Instead of handing out more tax money to convicted felons we should be thinking of how we can allow them back into society to lead a life that gives them a second chance. We should stop advocating for discrimination against this group of people in every walk of life. Right now, it is perfectly legal for any employer to turn away a job applicant based on his criminal record. After 9/11 almost every employer has been checking the easily accessible records of every job applicant.

Society should focus on the question of what to do with these people. Because if we don't have a solution for them they will have nothing to do except a continued life of crime. Tough talk and tough measures sell good to the electorate during elections but no politician dares telling the electorate that they are paying the ultimate price.

Last week, the local Detroit papers were filled with stories about ousted Detroit City Clerk, Jackie Currie, and that she had many people on her staff that had a prior criminal record, including her own son.

Yes, the public has the right to know about elected officials. But this open outcry in the media to exclude anyone with a criminal record from society is self-defeating. It will not lower the crime rate. A criminal record has become a "one strike you're out" system. One strike and you will become unemployable for the rest of your life. The British had a solution for this; two hundred years ago they sent all their convicted felons to a far-off place. Today, that place is called Australia.

December 3, 2005

Halal versus Haram: blessed versus sinful

He laid there lifeless in a casket and I stared at his clean-shaven face and his elegant suit. His name was Mike and he was a good friend. Last weekend he told me he was going to the hospital for his last session of chemotherapy. I talked to him Saturday and he sounded cheerful. He told me he would check out of the hospital for the final time on Monday. He did not lie. Monday morning he checked out for good as he relinquished his soul to the Prince of Death.

I stared at his lifeless body and remembered how I used to tell him "you're going to a place where worry does not exist." I recited Al-Fatiha verses from the Qur'an and prayed for God's compassion and forgiveness for his soul. He was a good man whose goodness touched everyone around him. I sat in the funeral home trying to look at the open casket but all I could see was lifeless matter and family members crying. I said to myself: this is Haram. This is not the way it's meant to be; a dead man should not be on display with lipstick and make-up and without his soul. We honor the dead by burying them without delay and without public display. They are shrouded in a white sheet and buried directly in the earth where they came from.

The same day I was invited to a wedding and I asked the young man if his bride was a virgin. He smiled and said: I only deal with Halal. I understood that the girl was never touched before by a man and the young man had gone through the necessary ritual of a Halal marriage contract.

I went to a Thanksgiving dinner the other day at my non-Arab relatives. An elderly lady commented: this is terrible we celebrate slaughtering the Indians and taking their land from them. I told her: No, we celebrate survival of the fittest and the triumph of the strong over the weak. She answered: so in a hundred years your great grandchildren will be celebrating with Israelis the slaughter of Palestinians? I said: you are right, this is Haram.

122

Very few non-Arab kids live on my street. But every Halloween young Arab kids dressed in all kinds of costumes knock on my door asking: trick or treat. A few years back I used to participate in this pagan tradition and I bought bags of chocolate just to give out to the giddy kids. A couple of years ago I stopped buying chocolate and last year I turned the porch light out as a signal to the kids to stay away. This year, Halloween came in the midst of Ramadan and I asked one of my neighbors if they'll let their kids dress up and go to houses. She said: No, it is Haram.

What is Halal and what is Haram? Halal is an act blessed by God and Haram is an act that God abhors and considers a sin. Most people see the sign Halal flashing in front of butcher shops and it means that cattle has been slaughtered in a Halal manner. It also means that they do not serve pork because eating the flesh of pig has been deemed Haram. It is a foul animal that feeds on its own faeces. We are what we eat and so we don't want to be like pigs.

Killing cattle in a Halal manner requires invoking the name of God, His mercy and having a very sharp knife to slice the animal's throat from the main vain all they way to the other vain. Blood must drain out of the dead animal before carving its meat.

Is the High School Prom Halal or Haram? That's a discussion a pious woman plans to initiate at Fordson High School. She is collecting signatures for a petition to stop this practice.

The concept of Halal and Haram is central to any faith. In Christianity it is the same concept of blessing and sin. But in Islam the concept is more pronounced as every action a person undertakes must pass this litmus test.

On April 24, 2003, President Bush declared victory in Dearborn to a large Iraqi audience. He finished his speech and turned around to shake the hands of people. He stuck his hand out to a head-covered woman but she did not shake it. He tried the next head-covered woman and she reacted the same way as the first one. He turned to the Mayor and asked: what's wrong why won't these women shake my hand? The Mayor answered: they are believers. The President said: I believe in God but I still shake people's hands.

Some body should have explained to Bush that some Muslim women consider shaking a strange man's hand as Haram, even if the hand belonged to Caesar himself. There is a wide gulf that divides east from

123

west and bridging this cultural gap will require both sides to meet halfway.

December 10, 2005

Doing business in Detroit

Owning real estate is a blessing of modern day freedom. But sometimes a piece of real estate in the city of Detroit can become a nightmare.

I bought a small industrial building a few years ago in Detroit to start a business with a partner. The business required parking space for customers. Adjacent to the building was an empty grass lot owned by the city. I went downtown and put in an application to purchase the lot. This was six years ago. I did not hear from them for a couple of years and so I went back again and resubmitted the application.

Again, I did not hear from them for another two years. I went back again and filled out a new application. This time I kept calling every month to track its progress in the labyrinth of the bureaucratic machine. I received a call in January of this year informing me that the City Council did not approve the purchase. I asked for a refund of my purchase money which was paid in advance a year earlier.

A couple of months went by and there was no check in the mail. I called again. They said that they were resubmitting my request to city council. This time they asked for a written statement of use. I wrote: it will be used as a parking lot for customers coming to the building next door. They called a month later saying that city council had asked "what was the building being used for?".

My partner had backed out of his end of the bargain early on and so I put a sign on the building "For Rent" or "For Sale". I wrote back to city council telling them that the building was empty waiting for a tenant. They wrote back telling me that the council would not approve the purchase till I had declared the usage of the building.

This is a classic chicken and egg stalemate; which came first the chicken or the egg? I called the employee and told her: this is a catch22 situation, I can not rent the building till I get some parking space and you won't allow me to have parking till I get a tenant, please send me my money back.

But by this point the city had become virtually bankrupt and city council was not eager to pay me back. They finally approved the sale 3 months ago.

It is very hard for a small business to make it in Detroit these days. As a business owner I find myself constantly fighting two enemies; thieves and government. I kept investing money in that building to make it attractive. A few months ago a brave tenant wanted to sign a lease but asked that I turn on the water service first.

I went downtown to the water department which is managed by the city of Detroit. I asked for the water to be turned on but they presented me with a $1,500 bill. I tried to contest the bill since there was no service or water used in six years. I talked to a supervisor who talked to her supervisor and finally at my insistence they talked to the top supervisor. I got a letter in the mail affirming the bill. I went downtown again and asked for a hearing with a third neutral party as I did not want to go to court over a water bill. They said I did not qualify for a hearing because I did not make any payments. I was stuck again with the chicken and egg stalemate. I insisted that there must be somebody somewhere in the water department willing to entertain a complaint. They said: send a letter to the Board of Water Commissioners. I did and I don't expect to hear from them for months, if ever at all.

This process began back in August of this year and I learned that nothing is ever simple when one deals with the water department. Some how the modern tools of efficiency, like the use of a credit card, have not reached this antiquated government utility. If you give them a meter reading and request a bill it takes at least three months. The employees have a combative attitude and just like one of the ads on TV they learned to say No to the customer.

This has been a tough year for the city of Detroit as it had to slash millions of dollars from its bloated budget. But instead of focusing their energy on cost cutting and making things easier for businesses, they shifted the burden to property owners. Instead of eliminating government waste they started issuing violation tickets to property owners, in order to generate the lost income.

The first one I received was called an "Annual Inspection" fee and it had a list of so-called violations. I figured clearing it would require months of wrangling with employees who had instructions not to listen, and so I saved myself the heartache and just paid it. Two months later I

125

got another $500 violation ticket for failing to cut the grass. But at the time I did not own the grass lot and my application was still stuck in city council. I tried to reason with the inspector to no avail. I paid it.

Two months ago I got a "Blight" ticket for $280. Last week I went to a brand new building downtown called "The Administrative Hearings Bldg" especially set up by the city for these tickets. I appeared before a city appointed lawyer who acted with full powers vested in a judge. I looked around and saw most of the property owners on my street. I was happy that this was not a conspiracy against me personally and that it targeted everyone equally.

The glorified magistrate was going through one customer after the other repeating the words of the inspector and telling us "it's the law". My turn came and I presented some sound arguments according to the building code. But she was a lawyer hell-bent on enforcing a code she hardly understood, and I found myself in the chicken and egg stalemate again. I paid the ticket as it was cheaper than having a heart attack.

I can't wait for the day when God sends me a buyer to liberate me from the nightmare of dealing with the city of Detroit.

December 17, 2005

Iran: the Sword of Islam?

The Middle East has become the land of the new gold rush. In the past two years revenues of some gulf nations have gone up more than five folds. The United Arab Emirates, Bahrain, Qatar, Saudi Arabia, Kuwait and even Iraq have become the new promised land of opportunity. Massive construction projects have started and new industries are springing up everywhere. It is the oil rush and it comes from increased demand for oil and natural gas. While here in America we are paying record prices for gasoline and heating bills.

American ingenuity and management expertise are being sought by these countries like never before. The economic connection between the Middle East and America has never been stronger. America has clearly won the war it went to Iraq to fight for.

Following the collapse of the US stock market in 2000 America needed a new fertile market for its products. America can export two things: junk products and management skill. In the arena of junk products

126

China has clearly taken the lead and has dominated much of the world markets. But American management know-how is still a leader in the world. That is the most expensive product that America can export.

The US could not stand idle watching Korean, Japanese, French and German companies take over the Middle Eastern market. It had to go to war to claim its territory and to cement its ownership of this market militarily.

Against this backdrop of unprecedented prosperity for the allies of America in the Middle East stands the threat of one of the axis of evil; Iran. The US has not taken any tangible steps to move towards a peaceful relationship with this nation of 70 million Muslims. The Iranian people view US policy in the region as anti-people and pro-oppression. The Iranian revolution in 1978 toppled America's hegemony in the region by removing its most ardent ally; the Iranian Shah. The US retaliated by supporting Saddam Hussein and his regime in an 8-year war of attrition to bleed this nation from its resources.

Iran survived and learned to become less rigid in its internal management. However, it has a great weakness which is the rule of the clergy over the people and its democracy is still in its infancy. Questions of morality still occupy most of their political dialogue while the majority of the people are impoverished. The regime is trying to build itself as a moral democracy concerning itself more with the behavior of women than accepting some of the good things that a commercial democracy can offer.

Earlier this year a man of the people who holds no title in the complex web of Iranian theocracy and against all odds was elected President of Iran. His name is Mahmoud Ahmadinejad and his rise carries a promise to make Iran the leading global voice of Islam. He was the mayor of Tehran and he rose in politics because of his competency in getting things done.

His approach is peaceful in nature but demands respect for the legitimate claims of Muslims around the world. The Bush administration figured that it would take over Iraq and from there it would spring its attacks on Iran and Syria. But they never got off first base. Iraq proved to be a nightmare and sewing it back together required the cooperation of Syria and Iran. But Syria and Iran can not afford to leave the Americans roam in peace in Iraq.

127

Recently, American public sentiment suffered a sudden loss of appetite for war forcing the Bush administration to scale back its hostile rhetoric. Iran kept its fingers in the Iraqi pie by the nature of the close ties that bind the Shi'a community. The Pro-Iran Iraqis kept pushing for a theocracy like Iran while the US pushed for a commercial democracy like its own. The end result enshrined in the Iraqi constitution was somewhere in the middle. The complex composition of the Iraqi population managed in the end to create a new animal called "commercial moral democracy". This new animal is tailored more for an "Arab" fit and so its progress began to affect the internal dynamics of Syria and Iran.

Iran's President Ahmadinejad recognized the new dynamics and like any democratically elected politician he began riding the wave of a new opportunity. Today he can afford to thumb his nose at the US and proceed with full speed in developing nuclear reactors. He keeps the lines of negotiations open with the Europeans because both parties can not afford to sever their economic ties. But at the end of the day Iran holds the upper hand if it decides to proceed unilaterally.

Regarding Israel which concerns every Muslim, Ahmadinejad dropped a bombshell last month by declaring that Israel must be wiped off the map. Last week he reacted to Austria's first payment of 200 million dollars to Jewish holocaust victims by urging sympathetic Europeans to give Israel a piece of land in Europe. He knows fully well that Europeans only gave Palestine to the Jews because they do not want Jews in Europe.

He added that Iran is prepared to recognize a government of Israel if it existed on European land. That is a compromise from his earlier position which indicates that his statements are intended mainly for two audiences. The primary audience of his speech is the far right in Israel and America, which only understands clear cut black and white "you're either with us or against us" type of statements. The secondary audience is the Muslim populace across the globe that will say: finally here's a leader of a Muslim nation who tells it like it is with no apologies. That's why he made his statements from Mecca so he may represent the prevailing sentiments of all Muslims.

Iran managed to improve its ties with the oil rich Arab states allied with the US and has put their fears of insecurity to rest. Iran is no longer interested in exporting dogma and has become focused on advancing the vital interests of all Muslims in the Middle East. Ahamadinejad's

128

statements strengthen the Palestinian side as they try to negotiate their independence from Israel.

His statements caused more discussion in Israel than in any other nation. We expect his comments on this topic to become more frequent as we get closer to Israeli elections scheduled for March 2006. I suspect that he wants to influence the outcome of these elections. His comments have so far strengthened the union of old Israeli generals namely Sharon and Perez. Their new party, the Kadima, rises in the polls as the threat of an external enemy increases.

The mind boggling question remains: why is Ahmadinejad helping Sharon get re-elected? Also, are those threats hollow intended for local Muslim consumption or will Iran ever dare to attack Israel? Waging an intense campaign of peace through strength might be Iran's ultimate objective.

December 24, 2005

A Christmas Story

The spirit of Christmas is all about giving and extending goodwill to others. It is a time of gratefulness, joy and sacrifice. Most of all, it is a time to knit broken relationships and to bond families together. It is a time of forgiveness. If a father had sworn not to talk to his son ever again, this is the time for the father to pick up the phone and call his son. If a daughter had run away from home, this is the time to pick up the phone and offer a line of connection.

It is that time of the year when we can reflect the bright joy in our hearts to the world outside. And it is not just in the form of bright lights and decorations, but in lasting deeds that change people's lives. If somebody asks for help don't shut them out. Just listen to what they want and do what you can; no more no less. If somebody owes you money and they can't pay exercise patience and give them a grace period.

This is the type of goodwill that does not cost any money but exacts a spiritual price. It is called sacrifice and it is an offering of one's own soul to the pond of the collective soul. If we all give a small drop it becomes a sea of goodwill. It creates a common spirit of goodness that can erase so much hurt and pain. It is the spirit of reconciliation and faithful love for the common bond of humanity.

129

A man believed in such goodwill. His parents died and he inherited lots of wealth. He went around giving much of his wealth to the poor and the needy. He gave his gifts in secret, and his wealth worked miracles in changing the destitute lives of many.

His name was Nikolaus and he lived in a town called Myra, in present day Turkey. He later became a bishop and he died in the fourth century. He became a celebrated Christian saint known as St. Nicholas. His legend survived the ages and about four centuries ago it was resurrected in the Netherlands under the name of SinterKlaas.

But the modern day image of Santa Claus did not develop till the latter part of the 19th century. In 1804, the New York Historical Society was founded and it chose St. Nicholas as its patron saint. Its members revived the Dutch tradition of St. Nicholas as a gift-giver. In 1821, a printer from New York named William Gilley published a poem about a "Santeclaus" who gave gifts celebrating the birth of the Christ child. His Santeclaus was a bearded man who dressed in fur and drove a sleigh pulled by one reindeer.

In 1823, another New Yorker, Clement Clarke Moore, published another poem entitled "An Account of a Visit from St. Nicholas". This poem put Santa's image on the literary map. Santa was given eight reindeer and he entered homes through the chimney.

Meanwhile, in many parts of Europe the image of the Christ child (or "Christkindlein") was overtaking St. Nicholas. Yet, there remained a Nicholas image accompanying the revered figure and he was referred to in France as "P'ere Noel".

At this point in Europe and in America, the symbols of the two personae began joining in a festive celebration of Christ's birth. Our secular Santa did not hit the big screen of stardom till Thomas Nast; a caricaturist for Harper's weekly, fully developed the pictorial image in 1866. Santa became the maker of toys and he was suited in the way we know him today.

In the 1930's Coca Cola hit a major slump in sales and so it recruited Santa as its commercial spokesman. He appeared in all of its advertising and his image was cemented in the public mind. The relationship brought Santa into every store, billboard and newspaper. It pushed Coca Cola to the top of soft drink sales. Over the next decades Santa found his way into every store, and had a hand in selling almost every product during the holiday season. And the rest is commercial history.

Well there you have it; the question on the mind of every child: does Santa Claus exist? A recent survey concluded that the majority of children's reaction after sitting in the lap of a real-life Santa was "indifference". Children can see through the creations of adults, but they will play along as long as they get what they want on the morning of December 25. The spirit of Santa is for adults while his gifts are for children.

My Christmas wish to everyone is that Santa brings them priceless gifts of the heart.

December 31, 2005

What's in store in 2006?

As we look back we find that human pain was the hallmark of 2005. I wonder if this trend will ease off in 2006, or will it escalate?

We love to celebrate the coming of anything new because it carries a promise of hope. A new born baby is a bundle of joy for a family as it brings with it renewed life. In the adult world, sometimes we experience life as a string of disappointments and regrets. In between these disappointments glimmers of hope push the forces of life forward. We look at a new baby and we see the promise of a better life than the one we've had. A new year is like a new baby. So, Happy New Year, and let's celebrate before it arrives and brings with it more misery.

I am trying to see the New Year as a "half-full" cup; from an angle of optimism. Yet, the pain of 2005 was too persistent to discount as an aberration, and most astrologers are forecasting more of the same. More natural disasters, more wars, more famines and more disease.

A lot of the pain inflicted upon us in 2005 by the forces of nature was in step with the pain that we seem resolved to inflict upon ourselves. The year started with a fuming tsunami that claimed the lives of more than two hundred thousand people in Southeast Asia. But the big natural disaster story that dominated the news was hurricane Katrina. The seas swelled up and exploded on the southern shores of America drowning the entire city of New Orleans. Then, we ended the year with an earthquake along the Pakistan-India border. It buried more than

87,000 people under its seismic fury and left millions others homeless and stranded in cold tents.

Insurance companies reported that they had their worst year ever where they paid a record $225 billion dollars to claimants. So, we can expect our insurance rates to go up in 2006. The government reported its worst budget deficit ever. So, we can expect our taxes to go up in 2006. Demand for energy was the highest reported to date. So, we can expect our heating bills and gasoline prices to go up in 2006. I am still looking at the cup being "half-full". It could be worse and so we must always be grateful for whatever challenges God sends our way.

We need to expect more pain in 2006 and in so doing any pain we receive less than the expected will be cause for celebration. It's all about managing expectations and this is especially true if you live in Michigan where Delphi declared bankruptcy this year, and American car-making is going through intensive care. Michigan will be lucky if this downturn bottoms out in 2006, but most likely it will be a long agonizing decline that may find a bottom in 2008.

I've always called America the land of extremes but it has a harsh dialogue of co-existence. Americans' hatred of Islam has reached new heights in 2005, but at the same time their acceptance of Muslims living amongst them has also reached a new height. Who can figure out the mother of all contradictions!

In Europe, London had its first encounter with Al-Qaeda terror but the city was no stranger to bomb attacks that plagued its streets for decades, as a result of the British occupation of Northern Ireland. Then, France witnessed ethnic riots for weeks unraveling the tragedy of social injustice. It is unclear whether unveiling Muslim girls in French schools had a hand in sparking off these riots. Similar types of unrest spilled over to other nations including Australia.

Hollywood has always played a leading role in the cultural education of Americans. For the longest time it painted a negative image of Arabs and their causes. The Kingdom of Heaven was the first movie to attempt a correction. Then, this year some blockbuster movies began to tackle the more intractable current issues. Syriana toyed with the issue of Middle Eastern oil. Paradise Now humanized suicide bombers, and Spielberg's Munich peeled off the label of terrorism to examine violence in the context of the Palestinian-Israeli conflict.

132

All three movies are nominated for major awards in 2006, and we should expect an explosion of such movies in the future.

This year the Neocons may learn to accept that democracy in the Middle East will yield results closer to the wishes of the people on the Arab street. And not their wishes. America may learn to stop hurting itself by making anti-democratic requests like excluding Hamas from the Palestinian elections. It may even take a sabbatical from its enrolment at the University of Israel where it obtains its primary schooling in dealing with the Middle East.

In Iraq, manmade disasters continued to claim the lives of people in yet more horrifying methods. But we had three elections and the last one attracted a record number of participants. We are on our way to establishing a democracy, even if it looks more like Iran's democracy. Our Neocon policymakers will insist on calling it a democracy even at the protestations of Saddam Hussein from his cage in court. He will not be found guilty and will most likely be exiled to a neutral gulf nation, and may end up a neighbor to Michael Jackson. I expect President Bush to declare yet another victory in Iraq in September 2006, as he begins to pull troops back in large numbers.

But this victorious pullback will come at the height of Bush's downfall. His descent from grace began this year, and that was probably the only piece of good news that we had to savor all year. The CIA leak scandal grew into a full blown justice department investigation which led to the indictment of the Vice President's chief of staff, I.Lewis Libby. It won't be long before the widely expected indictment of the architect of Bush's presidency, Karl Rove, will be announced.

The NSA's spying scandal will be on the front burner when the Senate reconvenes in January. Impeachment will be the Democrats' battle-cry as they head into the midterm elections of 2006. The good news is that we may live, God willing, to see the day when Bush will deliver the famous "I am not a crook" Nixon-like speech.

With all the pain that we must endure in 2006 there will always be the silver lining of Bush's downfall providing a flicker of hope that will make the future brighter than the past. Happy New Year.

Hamas: from terrorism to governance

US foreign policy focuses on the War on Terror. Palestinian Hamas has been classified by the State Department as a terrorist organization. Thus, on the face of it, it seems like a perfectly benign and consistent request when Secretary of State, Rice, calls onto the Palestinian Authority to exclude Hamas from the upcoming elections. But this is really the crux of the war on Terror, and it is a question whether the US wants to transform terrorist organizations into politically legitimate parties or whether it sees no place for them at all in its world order.

Hamas is not an organization like Al-Qaeda with a narrow base of support from eccentric individuals. Hamas has become part of the Palestinian mainstream and a request to exclude it is like excluding the Democratic Party from elections. Such a request reflects either extreme naïveté on the part of the State Department or a contradiction of its own policy of promoting democracy in the Middle East. But most likely, Secretary Rice acted on a request from the Israeli government.

We must operate under the premise that a democratic society is peaceful in nature. I assume that we are also operating under the assumption that democracy in the Middle East eliminates the threat of terror.

Bush's architect, Karl Rove, once said: the Democrats offer therapy to terrorists while we wage a war on them. But when terrorist organizations like Hamas campaign in the open for their ideas and win elections they become legitimate. They are legitimate in the eyes of their own people and the US can not ignore that fact. If we convince people that the ballot box is better than the gun then we no longer have a problem with terrorism. It's not about therapy. It's about policy-making. It is about Republicans hell-bent on waging a war with tanks and missiles or Democrats who can muster the courage to change failed policies.

The responsibility of governance pushes Hamas away from making suicidal decisions that impact the future of everyone. They become lawmakers and legislators in charge of the security and destiny of a people. They will most likely stop directing suicide attacks against Israeli civilians. This may happen when the Israeli government decides to stop its campaign of blowing up Hamas leaders.

Political terrorists act out of a deep conviction that they have made the ultimate sacrifice for their people. As long as people are occupied or oppressed there will be individual anarchists seeking liberty from the seemingly hopeless slow march of the collective. Elections offer a way out of hopelessness. The more people participate in an election the less support there is for individual anarchists to perform criminal acts, in the name of the people. Democracy is the way out of terrorism.

What's happening in Iraq today is very much different from what's happening in the occupied Palestinian land. Palestinian suicide bombers seek liberty from the ultimate oppression of Israeli occupation which has no end in sight. Al-Qaeda and Bin Laden attacked America because it supports Israel's oppressive regime. At the heart of the war on terror is the question of Palestinian liberty. America can not afford to sit on this issue, while pumping billions of dollars into a war in Iraq that does not address a legitimate grievance of why America became a target.

Ever since it was founded 18 years ago Hamas went the extra mile to prove to Palestinians that whatever money it collected it spent on the poor. It built shelters to house Palestinians who are constantly forced out of their homes by Israeli bulldozers. It built hospitals and offered free health care to all Palestinians. It established schools, homes for the orphans and supported widowed women.

Last month Hamas won over 60 percent of the local council elections. It had become an organized political party with a clear program for the electorate. It gained legitimacy because of its deep commitment to social work, clear political objectives and the failure of the Palestinian Authority to deliver on any promise.

Last year, Mahmoud Abbas campaigned on a platform of negotiations with Israel in order to achieve freedom. He was elected as the President and Hamas honored his platform by agreeing to a cease-fire. It halted its military operations and focused on strengthening its political base. Meanwhile, Israel did not offer Abbas anything to bolster his support. It continued building the wall of separation and gobbled up massive tracts of Palestinian land. The withdrawal from Gaza, last August, was unilateral and came from the Israeli side without negotiations. Israel could no longer sustain an occupation which had become too costly because of the military operations championed primarily by Hamas and Jihad.

The Palestinian people gave Hamas credit for the victory in Gaza. They rewarded Hamas in the latest local elections. Fatah headed by President Abbas failed in rooting out corruption from its ranks. It failed in delivering to the Palestinian people in most measures. But Abbas has been trying very hard to reform his party by offering an election slate full of younger names.

The old guard of Fatah is hanging onto power viciously and the issue of Palestinian voters in Jerusalem has put the legislative elections on hold for the time being. Fatah is breaking up from within and its slate for the new elections is headed by imprisoned Marwan Barghouti. Fatah is committing political suicide. Marwan will be elected because Palestinians respect his sacrifice, but he won't govern from his jail cell. Israel will be tempted to release him as it ponders the inevitable alternative of dealing with Hamas.

If Palestinian elections were held today Hamas will most likely gain a majority in the parliament. The next Palestinian government will be headed by Hamas and the US government will have to recognize it as a legitimate entity.

But the sudden heart attack suffered by Ariel Sharon changes the dynamics of Israeli politics profoundly. He was an apex of power who ruled from a wide base of support. His deputy Prime Minister, Ehud Olmert, will continue his march in the newly-formed Kadima Party, and Palestinian elections will stay put till Israel decides its new political fate in its elections in March.

Hamas stated this week that its cease-fire with Israel has expired and it has no intentions of renewing it. In response, Israeli Defense Minister, Shaoul Mofaz, offered to negotiate with Hamas provided that it laid down its weapons.

What remains certain is that this year Hamas will hold the key to the fortunes of all aspiring leaders in Israel and Palestine.

January 14, 2006

Dearborn Repair Bonds obstruct home ownership

It sits sad and abandoned devoid of the joy of life. A large faded sign through the window of the living room reads: HUD Home for Sale. The house had its days of glory but like our society had fallen into a

136

melancholic decline. It still does not understand why no one would move in it.

The house was probably built in the thirties and housed a new immigrant family that came to the land of opportunity. It was a small house with a big heart. Boys and girls grew up in it and then flew out of the nest. The couple that owned it aged and retired. The man died and the old woman lived alone for many years. Then, she died.

In the mid nineties a Lebanese investor bought it for $45,000. He gave it a cosmetic facelift and then sold it to a newly-wed Palestinian couple for $85,000. The couple tried for three years to have children to no avail. They blamed the house for their misfortune. The roof leaked and every time it rained the sewer flooded the basement. They complained of bone illness and spoke of strange spirits that haunted the house. The woman complained about her husband's abusive behavior and he accused her of being a lunatic. Finally, they divorced and the house was back in the open market.

The year was 2000 and it was the climax of the Clinton prosperity era. Dearborn was experiencing a real estate boom without end in sight. Young mortgage brokers sprang up every where and they had all kinds of twisted schemes up their sleeves. They sold the house to an Iraqi family that barely spoke English and got them stuck with a $105,000 mortgage. More than ten people lived in the two-bedroom home and the house was alive with the sound of children.

September 11 came and money began drying up. In 2002, the Iraqi man could no longer afford the monthly payments. He fought eviction till his country was "liberated" in mid 2003. Then, he concocted a twisted scheme of divorcing his wife on paper so that all his children will be eligible for welfare. The government moved his wife and children to a house in Detroit and he went back to Iraq. I heard that he married a young virgin in Iraq and I am not sure if he lived happily ever after.

Meanwhile, the house sat empty and the mortgage owner, the department of Housing and Urban Development (HUD), tried to sell it for $105,000. In Dearborn, you can not sell a house without a Certificate of Occupancy. City inspectors swooped into the house and wrote many pages of violations. Prospective buyers got copies of the inspection reports and placed their bids. The highest bid was $55,000 but HUD would not sell it.

A year later HUD dropped the asking price to $75,000 but the highest bid it received was $40,000. I was curious why no one would buy the house. I went to the city's Engineering and Safety department and examined the inspection reports. I estimated the cost of the work not to exceed $30,000. But the city required a performance bond of $60,000. It did not accept the kind of Bonds that could be purchased from Insurance companies. They required the prospective buyer to bring in a Cashier's check for $60,000 and hand it to the city. Then, they expected the owner to perform the work within a certain period of time, pass all inspections, and then come back to reclaim his money. The city wanted to guarantee that the owner actually performed the work. If he failed to do the work they would spend his money making the repairs themselves. No investor or home buyer is willing to hand the city $60,000 and give them the right to spend it.

This is the third year the house sits empty. Some squatters tried to move in and thieves keep hitting it. It sits as an eye-sore devaluating the entire block. HUD dropped its asking price to "please place a bid". I called the agent and asked what kind of a price they would accept. He said: $15,000. Still, no one would bid on it. The house comes with a huge liability that scares any prospective buyer. It is called the big stick of city government. No one wants to fight city hall.

Our building department wins over 90 percent of its legal cases. It stated to the media that it studies case-law regularly and tries to avoid the mistakes of other cities. It is a highly competent legal machine with resources that can outstrip any regular homeowner or investor. No one in his right mind would pick a legal fight with this department.

But I don't fault highly competent city employees for doing the best job they can. These employees have become too shrewd and too efficient in the service of a bad policy. The policy stifles growth of homeownership in Dearborn and discourages investment. The policy aims to have the city of Dearborn eventually gain the ownership of these homes through delinquent tax forfeitures. Then, the city will probably demolish them and sell the lots in an obscure manner at very low prices to friends of local politicians. This should not be an acceptable business practice.

Dearborn is like the country of Jordan; a prime beneficiary of wars and disasters in the Middle East. But peace is gaining ground in the Middle East and so demand for housing in Dearborn has slowed down dramatically after the "liberation" of Iraq.

138

The city should repeal its cash bond policy and allow people to buy homes that are still habitable. The current policy unfairly condemns many homes and sentences them to abandonment till they are vandalized beyond repair. You will find many of these abandoned homes with a red letter from the city pasted on the front door, and they are appearing in almost every block of east Dearborn.

This should be viewed as an opportunity by the local city council sworn in last week to serve another 4-year term. Many council members are involved in real estate and this should not turn into an opportunity to line up the pockets of their friends. This is an opportunity to deliver something of tangible value to the citizens of Dearborn, instead of just acting as a rubber stamp. It is time for Dearborn to wake up to the new economic realities of our state, and city council should focus on creating incentives to attract people to Dearborn.

January 21, 2006

Middle East Power Jockeys

Any political organization is a reflection of the ambitions of its leaders. The ceiling of their ambition determines how far their causes will progress. The primary jockeys of the events that will shape the Middle East in the short months ahead are Iran's President Ahmadinejad and his regional allies: Bashar Assad who heads the Syrian regime in Damascus; Sayed Hasan Nasrallah who heads Hizbollah in Lebanon, and Khalid Masha'al the leader of Hamas in exile.

The anti-thesis of this alliance is headed by US Vice President Dick Cheney; Israel's new Prime Minister Ehud Olmert, and Lebanese Druze leader Walid Jumblat. Now, there is a long list of other leaders sandwiched in between but some feel the heat more than others, like Saudi's King Abdallah and Egyptian President Mubarak.

In the world that exists in the mind of George W. Bush there are good guys in white coats and bad guys with machine guns wearing turbans. Bush's world was obsessed with Osama Bin Laden and Saddam Hussein. Since the demise of Al-Qaeda in Afghanistan and the dethroning of Saddam, Bush's world has been mired by incompetence, corruption, scandals and uncertainty. He started out 2006 by emphasizing that America is at war and terrorism is not a criminal activity to be handled by the justice system. But Bush's world has changed forever because his constituency has changed its priorities from war. Dick Cheney is more comfortable with the grey world of diplomacy and so he's taken over the affairs of the Middle East.

This past week he stopped in Saudi Arabia on his way to Kuwait where he attended the funeral of that country's prince. In Riyad he met with allies and had a frank conversation with Lebanon's new Sunni leader, Saad Al-Hariri. The political cauldron in Lebanon is boiling and could reach a critical mass soon and explode by this summer. America is pushing hard for disarming Hizbollah and it has strengthened the alliance of Jumblat with Christian leaders General Aoun and Dr. Geagea. The young Sunni leader, the son of slain former Prime Minister Rafik Al-Hariri finds himself in a precarious position holding the balance of power. He has recently gotten much closer to French President Jacque Chirac who had defined the interest of his nation in Lebanon through UN Resolution 1559 and its investigation of the Hariri murder.

The US has managed to exert extreme pressure on the Assad regime in Damascus in the past year. Syria withdrew all of its forces from Lebanon and its Vice President Abdel-Halim Khaddam has defected to Paris. The extent of Saad Al-Hariri's ambition is to exact revenge from the killers of his father and to preserve the vast wealth of his family. Revenge may lead to a civil war while wealth preservation requires peace. If he listens to Cheney's advice he will join the Jumblat alliance thereby sliding down a twisted path towards civil war. The target in the end is Hizbollah.

US policy sees that the demise of Hizbollah can have a domino effect in the region, where it may lead to the downfall of Hamas in Palestine. They both follow the same model in dealing with Israel and both consult closely with Tehran. The coordinated strategy between Hizbollah-Hamas-Damascus-Tehran has made steady and solid gains against Israel. Twenty years ago the frontline of military confrontation with Israel was near Beirut. Hizbollah moved it to southern Lebanon and in 2000 pushed the Israeli army behind the old border. It kept the heat on northern Israel and in Sheba'a farms at the foothills of the occupied Golan Heights.

Then, Hamas followed the same strategy with different tactics and pushed Israel out of Gaza. Today, home-made rockets are directed towards Netanya and Askalan. Israel cornered itself by building a massive wall of isolation so it can hide behind it, and has since abandoned its dream of a biblical land. The extent of the ambition of Ehud Olmert is to have a secure Israel inside the wall. Hamas now holds the key to his future. He is asking the Palestinian President, Abu Mazen, to disarm Hamas.

Abu Mazen is a pragmatist leader who was elected on a platform of negotiations with Israel and internal reforms. So far, he has failed on both agendas and he knows it. Olmert is trying to shore up Abu Mazen's Fatah party by pulling nine extremist families out of Hebron and opening the old town after 12 years of closure. He might also visit Ramallah as a symbolic gesture. Olmert has vested interest in Fatah's success in the elections next week. The target in Palestine is the same as in Lebanon; the weapons that can fight Israel.

The extent of Cheney's ambition in Iraq is to have political stability that would allow US troops to come home. The target is no longer defeating the terrorists. Iraq is in a state of civil war but no one wants to admit it.

The extent of Jumblat's ambition is to overthrow the Assad regime in Damascus and to become a major custodian of US interests in the region. He is the most ambitious of the Cheney-Olmert-Jumblat alliance. In the absence of an attractive alternative regime the US finds itself in no position to overthrow the Syrian regime. But at the same time it needs to keep it weak and constantly in a defensive posture.

Iran's Ahmadinejad spent two days in Syria this week bolstering the regime. The extent of his ambition is to wipe out Israel and to have nuclear power. His agenda is by far the most ambitious of all. He has taken the first bold step by removing the seals off the Natanz nuclear research facility and restarting the program unilaterally.

If Hamas wins the elections and Hizbollah manages to wiggle itself out of the Jumblat trap the US will be forced to modify its anti-terror policy in order to protect its wider interests in the region. Protecting Israel from any conceivable military threat may no longer become America's primary concern. That's when negotiations between Israelis and Palestinians may lead to a lasting solution to the conflict.

Palestinian Elections mark the birth of a nation

The results of the Palestinian elections show a clear victory for Hamas over Fatah. This week the Palestinians conducted for the first time in their history what can be considered a democratic election. The last time they went to the polls to choose their legislative council or parliament was almost ten years ago. Back then, Arafat and his Fatah Party had a monopoly on power by virtue of their Oslo accord with Israel. For the past ten years the Palestinian Parliament was virtually toothless and acted as a rubber stamp for the failed policies of the late Yasser Arafat.

The Palestinian people have been searching for peace since World War One when they were colonized by the victorious British. The British decided to give Palestine to European Jews to establish a state of their own. In 1947 the United Nations adopted a partition plan to establish two states living side by side. Arab regimes did not accept the plan and Israel established itself unilaterally in the war of 1948.

The Palestinian people have never had a vehicle or a political mechanism to assert their self-determination or exert a political will independent of the Arab states. Palestinian Prime Minister, Ahmad Qureia, recognized the importance of this election and said that it inaugurated a new era in Palestinian history. The big story in this election is basically Hamas. It is described as a terrorist organization by the US State department. Hamas has claimed responsibility for suicide bombings against Israeli civilians and has pledged itself to the destruction of the state of Israel. But Hamas has basically followed the model established earlier by Ben Gurion and the founders of Israel.

Respecting the sanctity of the lives of non-combatant civilians is a recent concept. The United States showed no such respect in its war in Vietnam. Every war has always targeted civilians indiscriminately and the term "terrorist" has been applied by one party to a conflict in order to dehumanize the other party. In the eyes of most Palestinians, the Israeli army is considered the greatest terrorist of all. The Israeli army uses jet fighters to bomb neighborhoods of Gaza. It bulldozes the homes of innocent civilians and assassinates Palestinians using state of the art helicopters.

Most Israelis now recognize that the occupation of Palestinians is terrorism in its ugliest form. They want out of occupation but they also want a harmless Palestinian state without independent borders and without an army that can defend it.

The ascendance of Hamas to power will actually enhance the chances for peace. Hamas campaigned on a platform of internal reform and armed resistance against the Israeli occupation. Fatah did not lose the elections considering its degree of failure. It managed to hold on to one third of the seats. Fatah's policy of negotiations with Israel has failed to bring any peace or prosperity to the Palestinians. Its monopoly over power has produced a class of corrupt leaders whose primary concern is achieving personal wealth.

For the first time in their history Palestinians have multiple political parties competing for their best interest. A democracy is always a work-in-progress. It is never perfect and it is never complete and its evolution depends on the level of dialogue and participation it solicits. This election witnessed the participation of over 70 percent of eligible voters. This high level of dialogue was always missing in Palestinian politics, and this election marks the birth of a nation. The hardest part of a democracy is establishing its starting point and setting in place a set of rules that guarantee a peaceful transfer of power. It took thirteen years for a handful of American founders to draft a constitution for the United States.

Establishing a democratic mechanism is the greatest struggle preceding the birth of a modern nation. This election marks the birth of a peaceful spirit of a nation. Hamas sought legitimacy from the Palestinian street championing the cause of clean government that can protect its citizens. It ran on a conservative agenda with rhetoric that can easily pass as Republican. But revolution and the responsibility of governance are two different things and it remains to be seen whether Hamas can make the transition that Fatah could never make.

Hamas has so far followed the path traveled by Hizbollah. It plans to pass a legislation that defines the borders of a Palestinian state unilaterally. That's where its agenda intersects with Israel's agenda. They are both in a race with time to define their borders unilaterally. Israeli Prime Minister Ehud Olmert stated this week that he will accelerate the completion of the separation wall. It is Israel's land grab in the eleventh hour before the declaration of a widely supported Palestinian state. He is campaigning for elections in March.

The Islamic Jihad Party which boycotted the elections declared this week that it had developed a missile with a 27 Km reach. The days of

143

suicide attacks are over when Palestinians can lob their missiles into the heart of Tel Aviv. Hamas can provide Israel with something it desires very dearly: security. But the price it will negotiate for that security will be the birth of a real nation.

February 4, 2006

Super Bowl: another quick-fix for Detroit

This is the biggest weekend Detroit will have in the spotlight for a very long time. The greatest sports event in the nation; the Super Bowl will be hosted in Detroit. It took a lot of hard work by a lot of hopeful people to bring this great event to the motor city. The city will shine in the limelight of celebrities and famous people who came to see the game. An estimated 300,000 people will be in the city for the super party weekend. More than 200 concerts will take place over the span of four days.

Everyone is going to benefit from this weekend to the tune of 1 billion dollars that will be spent by outside visitors. The money is a badly needed infusion of cash into the local economy. The Casinos stand to make the most money but hotels, restaurants and music halls will also get their fair share. Michigan has become a one-state recession while the rest of the nation enjoys the economic boom that Bush spoke about in his State of the Union address this week. Michigan has the highest unemployment rate in the nation and the gloomiest economic outlook.

Most celebrities and politicians will talk up Detroit and will spin it as an upwardly mobile city. Words of hope and optimism are intended to polish the tarnished image of a city that has fallen from grace. Half of the fans will come from Pittsburgh to cheer their team the Steelers. It is befitting that these people will get to see downtown Detroit as it may remind them of how their city looked like twenty years ago. Pittsburgh suffered from the collapse of the American steel industry. Just like Detroit is suffering today from the fast decline of the American auto industry.

For fifteen years people immigrated out of Pittsburgh seeking a livelihood elsewhere. Now, Michigan and especially Detroit is losing population at an accelerated pace. Pittsburgh was able to attract large banking and insurance concerns to revitalize its downtown. It focused on education and invested money expanding its universities. Some steel companies survived and became stronger than ever before.

144

Pittsburgh made the painful transformation to a diversified economic base, but it never resorted to sleazy business like gambling as a way out of its troubles. It confronted the problems head on and persevered in its pursuit of new life. But Detroit is addicted to the quick fix mentality and as much good press this Super Bowl hoopla will bring to Detroit, it is not enough to lift it out of its troubles.

I don't want to be the spoiler of this super party but it is like sugar candy. It offers very little permanence in its aftermath and will be forgotten as soon as the party trash is swept.

Detroit has to confront its problems head on and seek new life through the hard work of internal reform. What is the force of life, is it money or is it morality? I recently had a friendly discussion with a Detroit city official about the subject. I argued that gambling was a sickness and the introduction of Casinos in Detroit was its ruination. He could not defend the activity of gambling and called it a "Vampire" business yet he voted for the construction of casinos. He explained that without the revenues from Casinos the Detroit city government could not survive. I asked: what is so precious about saving an incompetent city government? He insisted that it was competent and worth saving. In my calculation the cost was too high for the benefit that humanity reaped.

He believed that gambling was a sickness just like drugs, yet he helped legalize the activity because it financed a defunct local government. Detroit is by no means a tourist town like Las Vegas attracting money from the outside. Most gamblers are local people who own businesses in the metro Detroit area. They sink almost 1.5 billion dollars a year into these casinos. This is money siphoned out of the local economy. This money could have gone into renovating abandoned buildings, buying new equipment and creating local employment. The local city government gets 17% of this revenue which finances 25% of its yearly budget. The end result is that the local economy loses over 1 billion dollars a year to save the jobs of 3000 city employees.

Let's ponder the other scenario for a moment and assume that morality is the main force of life and that money is a tool to achieve a moral purpose. Following the moral scenario would have kept almost 10 billion dollars invested in the local economy in the past seven years. It would have forced city government to shrink and cut one third of its size making it more in line with cities comparable in population. It would have kept thousands of people in honest jobs instead of

145

employing a handful as card dealer. Somebody should declare the Casino gamble as a failed adventure.

The glittering lights of Casinos tickle our addiction to the fanciful moment. Most of us refuse to confront the moral question that all this glitter is built on the destruction of people's lives. A house built on human misery can not stand. Detroit is still addicted to the pleasure of a fleeting moment and unless its politicians confront the hard moral questions it will be a ship floating aimlessly towards an inevitable wreck.

Party on Detroit and enjoy the Super Bowl moment. It is indeed very precious.

February 11, 2006

The Mother of all Cartoons

It is the cartoon that "broke the camel's back" so to speak. I really did not want to write about this issue because there is no winning in it. But it had become an international crisis and every person of conscience must now weigh in his opinion. This is an especially painful issue for us Arab and Muslim Americans. We fully appreciate both sides of the argument.

A cartoon project was commissioned by a Danish newspaper to criticize the Haram (prohibitions) in Islam and it developed into an issue of freedom of expression versus insulting Islam and its prophet. All across the Muslim world riots erupted from Indonesia to Iran to Turkey.

Muslim youths in Beirut watched what the kids were doing in Gaza and so they resolved to outdo them. Gazan kids took over the UN headquarters last week and showed their bravado to the cameras. Once the media was gone they went home giving up the building. The following day demonstrators in Beirut stormed the Danish embassy and torched it. Then the Syrians burned two embassies and just like the fuse portrayed in the cartoon it ignited all over the Muslim world culminating in Afghanistan where scores of people were shot dead and others wounded.

The escalating level of violence in places like Afghanistan has the undeniable imprint of the invisible hand of Taliban clerics who'd been

146

under siege since 9/11. They fanned the flames of ignorance and turned peaceful protests into violent mobs. How come Saudi Arabia, the supposed defender of Islam, has not permitted a single street demonstration? The poorest Muslims are the ones doing the most rioting. The cartoon has unraveled issues of poverty and despair that plague much of the Muslim world.

Who would've thought a cartoon would turn out to be mightier than the sword. Israel occupies by the sword Islam's third holiest site in Jerusalem while they sit idle, but a cartoon ignited their fury. It is a sign of the times we live in. Only those who pander to ignorance and use brazen force rule over the earth. Jerusalem has been cut off from the Muslim world for almost 40 years and thousands of cartoons by the most famous Palestinian cartoonist, the late Naji Al-Ali, failed to cause a single demonstration.

The Danish prime minister is partly to blame for this crisis. When the cartoon was first published last September, he snubbed the Muslim community who warned about the grave consequences. He refused to meet with them or with the ambassadors of many Muslim countries. When individual supermarkets in the Muslim world began boycotting Danish cheese and butter he offered a personal apology. Till today his country refuses to offer an official apology. He says that he is standing up for freedom of expression which is the bedrock of western civilization. But his country has a law which prohibits anyone from insulting Jews. The British government just sentenced a Muslim cleric, Al-Masri, to seven years in prison for inciting hate. So hating Muslims in the west is a right enshrined in its civilization while hating Jews is a crime. This hypocrisy is perfectly understood by most Muslims.

Denmark is a tiny country and it can not butt heads with Islam. The United States shied away from such a direct confrontation and the State department denounced the cartoons and urged a respectful interfaith dialogue.

Just like prophecies that drive religious zealots this was a self-fulfilling cartoon. I finally had to see it and figure out what the fuss was all about. Well it was a caricature of supposedly the Prophet Muhammad who looked more like a bearded angry Taliban figure wearing a turban that had dynamite in it with a lighted fuse.

The ticking bomb of Islam as portrayed in the cartoon exploded. The cartoon was published all over Europe as a way of defiance and solidarity with the Danish newspaper. It was no longer about religion or protecting freedom of expression. Europe stuck a needle in the eye of Islam to check if it hurts and whether Muslims have the guts to defend themselves. The issue is more about a clash of wills and who is more determined to change the ways of the other. Muslims need reform badly but they refuse to accept it from the western world.

The more pressure the west puts on them to reform the more they will retreat to militancy. I told a Rabbi recently that I did not like the sight of Burqas in Gaza and I was disturbed to see how women are being covered from head to toe. These sights are foreign to Palestinian society but moderation had brought them nothing but despair. If Palestinians become Talibanized I will blame Israel.

Butting heads with Islam forces it to become more radical and more militant. The more the west threatens Hamas, Hizbollah and Tehran the stronger they become. I know most of the western world disagrees if I tell them fighting with Islam is futile. The great majority of Muslims believe in their heart that humanity's salvation lies in the Qur'an.

I checked the pulse of America and surveys have shown that two thirds of Americans thought it was acceptable to publish the "Muhammad Cartoon." Here's what some people had to say on internet message boards:

"If we believe that "freedom of the press" means freedom to insult a specific group over another, then we should all have the same freedom to insult any group we want no matter who they are, and then let's see where all this insulting leads us".

"It was a foolish thing to mock a religion with a cartoon. Any religion. The reaction also cannot be excused."

"What an insane group these people are. I think instead of editorial cartoons, they be be-headed. Those people seem to accept that. A cartoon? Oh no, how dare you."

"The United States needs to develop a fuel to replace oil. We can put the Middle East out of business. Then that region of idiots can kill themselves until their hearts content. The cable stations could telecast Jihad Fest and we could watch these jerks jump up and down chanting, burning, and killing."

148

No two wrongs can ever make a right. The insult is wrong and the violent reaction is wrong. But any self-respecting human being would react to an insult with indignation. Denmark can not expect to have its economy supported by the people it insulted. This will break the back of the Danish cow, and if street sentiment begins to dictate national policies the Danish Prime Minister may have to offer his resignation.

I also checked the pulse of Arab Americans. In various discussions I discovered that their reaction was typical of a community stuck in the middle of two cultures. They saw that both sides were right and both sides were wrong. But most of all they did not want to be involved in this no-win situation. Unlike their poverty-stricken brethren in the Muslim world they had something to protect; the American dream.

February 18, 2006

The Hariri Legacy

This week marked the first anniversary of the assassination of Lebanese leader and former Prime Minister Rafik Al-Hariri. Half a million Lebanese people gathered in Liberty square in Beirut on Tuesday, February 14, to commemorate the occasion. Druze leader, Walid Jumblat focused his speech on the evils of the Syrian regime and called Syrian President Bashar Assad a terrorist. A month ago he stated to the press that he considered the Syrian regime as his enemy and not Israel.

Many Druze leaders from Syria and Palestine were quick to denounce Jumblat's name-calling and to distance themselves from the renegade leader. But his point of view still garners considerable support and most notably he is allied with Saad Al-Hariri, the son of the slain leader and heir to his throne. He spoke to the fervent crowd and echoed sentiments of independence from Syria and its influence.

A week earlier he was in Washington, DC, where he met with President Bush and received instructions on how to navigate through the next critical phase of Lebanese politics. In the past six months he spent most of his time in France because he feared for his life. Many Lebanese leaders who spoke against Syrian interests in the past year have met with the Hariri explosive and deadly fate. These coincidences add up to a pattern and the Syrian regime is still hanging on to dear life.

The dictatorship in Damascus obtains legitimacy because it is the last Arab holdout against Israel. It has avoided deep internal reforms

149

because of its popular position against Israel. Israel's warmongering existence has been a nightmare crouched upon the breast of Arabs and Muslims. It exists to make war in the region and to prop up corrupt regimes opposed to the will of their people. It is a complicated formula that makes Arabs tolerant of the Syrian regime.

But Saad Al-Hariri's alliance with Jumblat goes against the current tide of politics in the Middle East. His father was a pragmatic politician who knew how to unite conflicting interests. Even the Sunni population in Lebanon that is represented by Saad and his party is moving closer to a natural alliance with Hizbollah. The tide of Hizbollah-Hamas-Syria-Iran is gaining ground at a much faster pace than the US-Israel tide. The Jumblat-Hariri alliance is betting on the military might of the US-Israel tide and has called for the resignation of Lebanese President Emile Lahood.

Rafik Al-Hariri was a shrewd businessman. He romanced the US-Israel tide but never joined it against his own people. He took lessons from history and rarely made enemies in the Arab and Muslim world. Saad has placed all of his eggs in the US-Israel basket and sought the protection of the monarch in Saudi Arabia.

His father had a knack for wealth creation and he made sure he also enriched the people around him. He arrived in Lebanon in 1992 after leading a very successful career in Saudi Arabia where he amassed a five billion dollar fortune. As Prime Minister in the nineties he instituted free market policies and took out one loan after the other from western nations to finance the reconstruction of a country devastated by 15 years of civil war.

His entry to Lebanon was facilitated by the Syrian regime in Damascus and it was his strongest ally for the longest time. Even when differences began to surface he was careful not to offend the Syrians. By the time he was killed his fortune was estimated at 25 billion dollars and his country, Lebanon had become one of the greatest indebted nations in the world.

Lebanon's external debt is estimated today at 37 billion dollars while its yearly GDP is 17 billion. The government spends almost 30% of its budget servicing the debt or paying interest to foreign investors. Most of the infrastructure projects that the Lebanese government paid for somehow benefited Rafik's personal investments. He was a man who cared about his country the way an investor carefully nurtures a privately-owned estate. It was never about a people, ideology, land or

150

convictions. He had learned from his royal Saudi relatives how to run a profitable plantation. Most countries in the Middle East are structured the same way. Nonetheless, he sought to unite people and find a framework of co-existence.

Lebanon stands today at a critical juncture and it could turn into a failed enterprise by the heavy burden of its debt. The current government must accelerate its economic liberalization to stimulate a higher rate of growth. But it is bogged down by internal squabbles and how to integrate Hizbollah's military into a national defense force.

Saad Al-Hariri's primary objective is to protect his family's fortune and avenge his father's murder. But he lacks his father's wisdom. He managed to corner himself and to become a committed side to a brewing conflict. He has disgraced his father's patriotic legacy by joining hands with the eccentric Jumblat.

The project of Lebanon's independence from Syria was championed by the French colonists. They gave it independence in 1946 and imposed a sectarian constitution that empowered Christian Maronites. Lebanon's claim of independence is the product of a French-Maronite alliance. Thus, it was particularly important for Hizbollah to find a popular Christian ally other than President Lahood. General Michel Aoun who has presidential ambitions fit the bill and he decided to break away from the traditional Christian forces and enter into an alliance with Hizbollah.

The unholy alliance has sparked a refreshing debate about amending Lebanon's constitution to a one-man one-vote system where any citizen can run for president. Religious discrimination has always been the basis of Lebanon's political structure and it was deliberately designed to always be a fragile coalition between different sects. The Lebanese can free themselves from the Syrian regime but they will never be truly free until they liberate themselves from their sectarian constitution.

The Hariri assassination has moved Lebanon closer to independence and by a twist of fate his death could result in real freedom for the Lebanese people. In the past year the Syrian military withdrew from Lebanon and Syria agreed to draw internationally-recognized borders with Lebanon which include the occupied Sheb'a farms.

It remains to be seen how history will remember Rafik Al-Hariri and whether his legacy will be defined by the reckless choices of an inexperienced son.

February 25, 2006

Selling US Seaports to Arab Terrorists!

Dave Ross is a radio broadcaster for the CBS radio stations network which airs his opinion nationwide. He usually tries to strike a balance in his commentary so as to inform and not to inflame. But here's what he had to say the other day: "the nineteen hijackers who attacked America on 9/11 were all Arabs. Two of them are connected with the United Arab Emirates. We are selling 6 of our seaports to the United Arab Emirates. Does this pose a security risk? Sure, it does. It doesn't take a genius to figure that one out."

Maybe Dave Ross did not say it but he made a strong implication that every Arab is a terrorist. The implication is as clear as sunshine but playing with the words in order to sound politically correct is something the media has gotten good at. But I don't blame the media for spreading fear and sometimes going the extra mile to sound an alarm. That's the nature of commercial news. It needs to be attention-grabbing in order to sell.

The American media is always looking for an easy story to report, that is short on details and far-reaching in magnitude. It tends to oversimplify because it believes that the general public has little tolerance for depth. The media masters the science of naiveté. Its conclusion, however, is backed up by surveys, data and consumer viewing habits.

They also know that the people who care about national security issues are mostly to the right of center. They are the so-called "Reagan Democrats." They are the ones most likely to write to papers, call up media outlets, contact their congressman, donate to political parties, and most importantly they tend to vote.

This story has gained traction and it took the White House by surprise. The Treasury Department approved the deal last month after scrutinizing it the same way it does other commercial arrangements. What is the story here? Why did it make such big headlines so fast? The media cried foul when it heard the word Arab taking charge of a US entry port. The media framed the story in such a way that alarms the average American who has little tolerance for depth.

First of all, US seaports are not bought or sold. They are owned by the federal government and the Department of Homeland Security will

152

always be responsible for security at these ports. The US government leases cargo handling to shipping companies because they can run a more efficient operation. A London-based company by the name of Peninsular and Oriental Steam Navigation, also known as P&O, was recently bought out by Dubai Ports World. P&O has a lease to handle cargo operations at 6 US seaports; New York, New Jersey, Philadelphia, Baltimore, New Orleans and Miami.

P&O sold this lease along with cargo handling management contracts for seaports all over the world including two ports in Britain, one in Australia and many others in Southeast Asia. It is a purely financial deal championed by the Prince of Dubai, who owns Dubai Ports World. Most of the personnel who currently run American operations for P&O will remain in their positions. They all have special security clearances and any new personnel added will have to obtain the same clearance.

Administration officials including President Bush have defended this deal vehemently and they are sticking to their guns. Bush threatened to veto any legislation from congress that attempted to block the deal. But this is an election year and Democrats are desperate to weaken Bush on the national security issue. I can picture the TV ads already. It will have sad music and aerial shots of the seaports of New York and New Jersey with commentary that may go like this: "they attacked our nation on 9/11"- pictures of 19 Arab faces appear on the screen- "Bush and the Republicans turned over our seaports to them so they can be in charge of our security"- a video of a fox in a hen house- "this is the Republican plan for Homeland Security."

The Bush administration has shown honest incompetence in handling major issues but on this particular issue I commend President Bush for his position. The criticism he faces comes from a sick implication that all Arabs are terrorists, and it has nothing to do with a security risk. President Bush and his entire team have faced this criticism head on and with refreshing candor. I rarely admire what Secretary of Defense Donald Rumsfeld says, but on this occasion he showed that he was disturbed by the media and its implication that all Arabs are terrorists. He said that the UAE was one of the strongest allies in the war on terror and that "we picked up some American citizens in our war in Afghanistan."

This is a rare occasion where we should stand firm with President Bush and tell our friends in the Democratic Party: if you stoop to race-baiting you will not only lose this election but you will also lose your soul.

It is time to boycott the Detroit News

The Detroit News published its official position regarding the Palestinian elections through a column written by its editor Nolan Finley on February 5, 2006. The column received a lot of attention from the Arab American community as it bashed Palestinians and said that terrorism is an "inseparable part of the Palestinian identity."

Many organizations moved to demand an apology from the Detroit News and community members sent letters in protestation. But the Detroit News insisted on its views and made further intractable justifications for its position. I wrote them a letter the day the column appeared. It said:

"Dear Editor,

Your views are extremely biased and uncritical of Israel. Obviously, you have never lived under the conditions of a foreign military occupation. I suggest that you invest a little time in learning about a subject before using your position to pander to your masters. You describe the Palestinians as a people whose "lust for Jewish blood is stronger than their desire to lead peaceful, secure lives, to rule an independent state, to lift themselves out of their misery."

These are ignorant statements that serve to dehumanize another people whose only crime is trying to regain their own homeland. Democracy strengthens a people's resolve for freedom and the Palestinians have resolved to defend themselves, create a state of their own and to have an effective government. All these goals intersect with the interests of Americans.

Although I appreciate why you need to pledge yourself again to the Zionist cause but your views will not help Israel achieve peace or find acceptance in the Middle East. The Palestinians live under extreme conditions of poverty and despair caused by a 40-year old occupation. They have been very patient waiting for the world to find a solution and all they get is the kind of rubbish that you write. Peace will begin the day occupation ends. Let's focus on ending the occupation as soon as possible if you are so eager to serve Israeli interests."

Nolan Finley represents the views of a huge news organization. It is the official position of a paper and he states very clearly and in bold

154

letters that "Terror defines Palestinians." They have a point of view which we happen to disagree with totally. Their size and market dominance will always frame the terms of this debate. They have no need to change their position because we do not present a threat to their interests. Thus, they will keep feeding us their rotten views and forcing us to pay for them.

I am personally not surprised by their characterization that "Terrorism is the history of the Palestinian people, and it will be their future..." The Detroit News has been consistently saying the same thing for many years while we tried to reason with its editors to no avail. They offer no solutions except further isolation of Palestinians and more collective punishment by cutting off all aid in order to starve them further.

They demand that Palestinians become democratic, tolerant and to establish an open and pluralistic society. That's exactly what every Palestinian wants too. There is agreement on the objective but there is an incredible disagreement on how to get there. Their "Roadmap to Peace" legitimizes the right of occupation to ensure Israel's security. Our roadmap to peace legitimizes the Palestinian right to resist a foreign occupation. Israel wants America to equate any resistance to occupation as terrorism and the Detroit News faithfully broadcasts this view. Israel's policies of further imprisonment and closing of the occupied territories will only lead to a more closed and desperate Palestinian society.

They demand openness while they force closure. They demand tolerance while they starve 4 million people. They demand peace while they assassinate, bomb, and invade Palestinian towns every day. They demand love while they exercise destructive hate.

They want the world to help them hold down the Palestinians to the ground while they keep beating them. Israel's lust for Palestinian blood is insatiable. Its very existence lacks a moral basis and so it must always be at war with Arabs and Muslims. Peace is the enemy of Israel. Warmongering has been the heartbeat of its survival and Sharon was a man who really understood that. Israel will never sign a peace agreement with Palestinians so long as there is one dispossessed Palestinian who claims that Haifa is his home.

What's the bottom line? If you have sheer force then your opponent will respect you. Palestinians have gotten nothing in the past dozen years of peace negotiations because they lack an organized resistance movement with legitimate targets and systematic methods. Most

Palestinians do not like the idea of suicide bombers who kill themselves and kill other Israeli civilians just to spread terror and insecurity.

We constantly find ourselves in a position trying to explain the reasons that drive such people to such desperate acts. But after 9/11 America has basically closed its ears. Most Americans think of the parallels between 9/11 and a suicide bomber in Israel and sympathy goes to the Israeli victims. The world has changed after 9/11 because of the horrific magnitude of the attack and the lack of justification.

Arab Americans disagree with suicide bombing as a legitimate tool to resist occupation. So why defend it? I don't. I am not an apologist for terrorism but at the same time I don't want the Detroit News to paint Palestinians with a broad brush that they are all terrorists because they elected Hamas. The News claims that "Hamas is no different from Al-Qaida" thereby reducing the Palestinian cause to a despotic terrorist movement. Therefore, it leaves us with an unspoken conclusion that America must help Israel kill all Palestinians.

Since I am alive and I still have a shred of self-respect, I am therefore obliged to fight for my right to live a dignified life like any other human being on this earth. The Detroit News is clearly opposed to that notion and it propagates the idea that Palestinians are a threat to the civilized world. I am obliged then to take every peaceful step within my power to snuff out its existence as a profitable enterprise.

Every Arab-owned gas station should throw out the Detroit News from its store. Every self-respecting Arab American should cancel his subscription to this paper. The Detroit News deserves no support from any peace-loving human being. It must retract its words and issue a clear position calling onto Israel to end the occupation as the only solution to resolve this conflict.

Until then, we must ignore the existence of this paper and stop all our dealings with it.

Peaceful Economic Wars

How can wars be peaceful? In the corporate world business is war. It is a daily struggle to make a profit, to manage people effectively and to create products that people want. It is also a war in the free market where fierce competition makes survival of the fittest a reality. These commercial wars spill over to legislation where lawmakers are enlisted to protect the interests of profitability. Politicians turn into brokers who get paid for legislating favorable laws. That is the nature of a commercial democracy such as the one we live in.

Economic wars are painted as legitimate because they are peaceful in nature and each party tries to strangle the livelihood of another party, all within the law. Right now, we are experiencing a rage of economic wars. Arabs and Muslims are increasingly under an economic siege here and abroad. Americans in the corporate world are increasing the daily cooler snipes like "they come to our country and buy up our gas stations and then build palaces at home."

We have been dealing with ignorant statements like "why don't Arabs pay taxes" and "the government gives them money to buy their own business" for as long as I can remember. But what saves us is our conviction in the American dream and our personal initiative. The Arab American economy is largely enterprise-based and self-reliant. It can stand on its own merit and demand respect for its contribution and flex some muscle for a change. It can slap temporary sanctions against shameless institutions, like the Detroit News, that constantly demean it.

The recent media outcry against a Dubai company taking over cargo handling at 6 US seaports has opened the floodgates of open discrimination against Arab businesses. This is commercial discrimination and it is as ugly as any other type of discrimination. The only difference is that it is being championed by the Democrats. They have an honorable history of opposing discrimination, but now they are igniting an economic war that promises to widen the divide between Muslims and Americans.

Economic sanctions have become the primary tool of diplomacy. Regular people on the street are doing it by boycotting certain products. Companies are doing it by excluding Arabs from their employment and the nation is doing it as a matter of policy. But America has opened the eyes of other nations to a weapon that can be used against it.

Venezuelan President Hugo Chavez is up for re-election this year. He is telling his people that the US government wants to remove him by force. It should not come as a surprise if he decides to cut off oil exports to the US. This will send the American economy into a tailspin worse than the 9/11 recession. America imports 5 percent of its oil from Venezuela and such a move could spike gas prices to 5 dollars per gallon at the pump.

President Bush has finally awakened to America's energy vulnerability, and has made independence from oil and fossil fuels the platform of his 2006 presidency. He just came back from India where he concluded a bilateral nuclear energy agreement which turned a blind eye to India's nuclear weapons. It is a fact that America's interest lies in reducing global dependence on oil. And it should have been done years ago instead of waging real wars, like the one in Iraq, for oil.

But economic and so-called peaceful wars promise to escalate and to pose a bigger threat to world's security than terrorism. They are plunging more than half the world's population into abject poverty and despair. The current order only recognizes one super power with super profit ambitions while the rest of the world must fight tooth and nail for survival. International law is being circumscribed to serve the interest of global corporations. American foreign policy is misguided in the belief that it can sanction others, while other nations are not allowed to retaliate with their own sanctions against America. A determined coalition of the dispossessed is emerging as a united front and it includes North Korea, Cuba, Venezuela, Iran, Syria, South Lebanon (Hizbollah), and the latest entrant; occupied Palestine. But those who sympathize with the dispossessed number in the billions from Malaysia to Morocco to Bolivia.

In the name of fighting Hamas Israel is choking the livelihood of every Palestinian. It has sealed off the Gaza strip completely and stopped all Palestinian products from going anywhere. Gaza is under siege by sea, land and air. Now, Israel wants to cut off their water, electricity and oil, and kill their new Prime Minister, Ismail Haniya. Economic isolation of designated "enemy" nations will lead to more resistance. It is the natural reaction of any human being whose bread was taken away from him.

Threats against Iran are escalating and its nuclear program has been referred to the UN Security Council. Iran will soon retaliate by suspending oil imports to the West. This will shake world markets and the price of oil will jump to $100 per barrel. But before it makes such a

158

big move Iran will keep the threat alive for months in order to shake the US economy and its financial markets.

Most oil producing Arab nations have ceded the power of their economies to America. They have become toothless when it comes to exercising political muscle that comes with economic power. The oil embargo option was taken away from them after the death of King Faisal in 1975. Their money can not buy them respect or independence. Our local community here is stuck in the same rut of being too scared to rock the boat, and to oppose American forces that hate their existence.

If Arabs and Muslims do not learn how to use the political clout that comes with their economic resources they will never win a peaceful war.

March 18, 2006

Stories of crime and punishment

He was a peaceful man who minded his own business and had a small store to earn a living for his family. One day he had an argument with his wife and he hit her. She called the police. He was handcuffed and removed from his house. He sat in jail for a few days and then appeared before a judge. His lawyer advised him to plead guilty and he didn't know what he was pleading to except that if he said the magic word he would be out of jail. He was out of jail but received a 2-year probation sentence and was told not to go home. The judge had slapped a Personal Protection Order (PPO) and he was not allowed to come within a 100 feet of his house. He could not see his children and he was summarily separated from his wife of 18 years. She forgave him but he could not talk to her face to face.

That's the story of the immense inequities in our justice system. It works to separate a man from his wife and children instead of reconciling differences and helping people come together.

Another man wanted to collect rent from a delinquent tenant. He relied on these proceeds to keep up with his mortgage payments but his tenant stopped paying rent for 3 months. He went to the house and banged on the door and told the tenant who was a single woman to pay up or face eviction. As he walked across the street a police car approached speedily and came to a screeching halt. Two police officers jumped out of the car and called out his name. He looked astonished but acknowledged the person they called was he. They jumped him to the ground and plowed his face into the asphalt as they handcuffed him. He was thrown in jail for a week before he appeared before a judge. He was charged with assault, trespassing and making threats to inflict bodily harm. The prosecutor offered him 6 months in jail in a plea bargain. He insisted on his innocence and requested a trial.

After 3 months in jail his trial began. The tenant was the main witness and it boiled down to her word against his. His lawyer advised him to plead out as the jury was more inclined to side with a tenant against a landlord, especially if the tenant was a white woman and the landlord was an Arab. The prosecutor offered him another deal that reduced his jail sentence to the time he had already served. He took the deal and was released the next day. He received a 2-year probation sentence and a criminal record. Meanwhile, he was suspended from his job at a factory and his house was under bank foreclosure proceedings. The tenant applied for a PPO and it was granted by the judge. So, our landlord could not come within 100 feet of his house to ask for rent.

The tenant had won in evicting the landlord and denying him the right even to ask for rent. Of course, with the help of the great justice system. The last time I talked to him he was ecstatic that the bank had listed his house in a foreclosure sale. It did not matter that his credit was ruined and it did not matter to him that he was no longer employed. He was happy because in a roundabout way that ruined his life the tenant was finally getting evicted.

Another man was addicted to gambling and it was ruining his life. He signed a paper at the casino asking them not to let him enter the establishment again. Three months later his will power weakened and he found himself betting at a roulette table. Within five minutes two security officers escorted him to a jail cell at the upper level. A state trooper came a half hour later and asked him questions and filled out a report. He was released and a month later he received a criminal citation from the Attorney General's office charging him with trespassing. At first he thought it was a joke but the seriousness of the charge dawned on him as he was formally arraigned and brought in front of a judge for a bond hearing.

He complained to me that he had carried out a voluntary act to cure himself from a disease and the justice system was punishing him. He faced up to six months in jail, fines and probation. Worst of all he was faced with the prospect of accruing a criminal record that shut out many doors of opportunity. If an alcoholic showed up at an AA (Alcoholic Anonymous) meeting does he expect to be arrested? He pressed me for an answer. It was truly an odd story. There ought to be a law that encourages people not to gamble and if they ask for help they should find counselors at casinos instead of police officers.

Therapy is not the work of the criminal justice system and no person was ever corrected by a probation sentence. The state of Michigan entrusts probation to the "Department of Corrections" and what a misnomer that is. I have yet to meet a "corrected' person who went through the system. The name attempts to justify the hefty salaries of an army of useless bureaucrats.

There ought to be a "complaint box" at every court building where people can make a complaint to someone about the inequities of the justice system. It is a novel idea but why does it need to be so hard-nosed and why does every judge have to act like Caesar?! It is a very tough system that shows no understanding for any circumstance and has no respect for anybody's time. It does not hear complaints and the only way to correct it is by exhausting enormous amounts of resources in higher appeal courts.

A good man loved his daughter but not her mother. He paid child support religiously for many years and then he lost his job. His child support payment as calculated by the court and according to his income was $750 per month. He filed for unemployment benefits as he looked for another job. He received a $1000 per month while unemployed. He went to "friends of the court" to tell them that he can not afford to pay $750 for child support and asked for a hearing. They gave him a date six months away. Meanwhile, they told him if he failed to maintain the current payment amount a warrant for his arrest would be issued.

Two months later he could not send a child support payment as he had a family of his own to support. But he was arrested and thrown in jail. He pleaded guilty to failing to maintain child support payments. Now, he is on probation with a criminal record looking for a job. What purpose did this serve besides pleasing the Attorney General who is constantly gloating over his stellar record of prosecuting "dead beat" dads.

An unabashed thief stole a car from a dealership in the middle of the day. He almost killed the salesman who was standing in front of the car. Luckily, a police car chased him down the street. He turned a sharp corner and crashed the car into a light pole. He was arrested and taken to jail. A week later he was released after pleading guilty and receiving a 3-month probation sentence.

It is time to reform this senseless justice system that treats most people like they are hard-core criminals. And treats hard-core criminals with great understanding and civility.

March 25, 2006

Time to end the occupation of Iraq

They say that one eventually becomes what he despises the most. Teenagers who swear that they will never become like their parents grow up to find themselves repeating the words of their parents to their own teenagers. The cycle of life catches up with everyone lifting youthful civilizations up and sending older ones to their graves. The American civilization is going through its natural life cycle and its transformation to an imperial democracy would make George Washington turn in his grave. America stands today for everything his revolution opposed.

If Washington lived today US foreign policy would have his revolution classified as a terrorist organization. He opposed occupation and led a resistance movement to fight British troops. He ambushed soldiers and blew up British supply lines. He received aid from an unfriendly foreign nation, France, and propagated an ideology of independence.

This week marked the third anniversary of the Iraq war and it was highlighted by anti-war demonstrations all over the world and pro-war speeches by President Bush and Prime Minister Blair. They have a plan for success and a strategy for victory. Bush spent the better part of this week explaining his strategy and reminding the nation that this is a major part of the global war on terror. He described the terrorists as "Islamo-fascists" with a totalitarian ideology that they want to impose on the rest of the world.

His strategy is simple: kill the terrorists, train the Iraqi army, form a new Iraqi government and then everything will fall into place. As to part one: the terrorists, Bush won't listen to anyone who tells him that "there is plenty more of where they came from." The more Arabs are killed whether they are terrorists or not the more bad blood ensues and that leads to more recruits for terrorism. A conservative estimate puts

162

the death toll of Iraqis in the past three years near 50,000. The terrorists are classified into three groups: Saddam loyalists and their Sunni supporters; foreign terrorists consisting of Zarqawi, Al-Qaida and their gangs; and Shi'a terrorists manipulated by Imam Muqtada Al-Sadr and Iran.

The terrorists just can not be simply killed because they are a direct function of the foreign occupation. Anyone who subscribes to the idea that occupation leads to peace is just simply wrong. Freedom is by far the strongest instinctual aspiration of every human being. Occupation creates resistance. Therefore, peace begins the day occupation ends. The longer American troops stay in Iraq the worse things will get. Foreign troops remain the core of the problem.

Former Iraqi Prime Minister, Iyad Alawi, stated this week that Iraq was in fact in a civil war. Sunnis, Shi'a and Kurds and all others have lived in that part of the world for thousands of years. They will use sectarian violence to advance their own narrow agendas for a limited period of time while they jockey for power. But the fabric of society will not tear if American troops withdrew today. Most of the sectarian infighting that we see nowadays will disappear soon after the occupying troops leave.

As for part two of Bush's strategy: train the Iraqi army to take over. Paul Bremer dismantled the Iraqi army in July 2003 thereby sparking off the insurgency. Now, they are accelerating the recruitment process and trying to fix what they broke by bringing back some of the experienced soldiers they had alienated. And part three of Bush's strategy which is forming a unity government depends on the approval and full participation of Iran. Bush stated that he instructed his Ambassador Zalmay Khalilzad to "inform" the Iranians of the American position. Iran's elected loyalists in the Iraqi parliament are prepared to block the formation of a new government indefinitely. The US has no choice but to negotiate with Iran on the formation of a new Iraqi government.

What did America accomplish in the past three years in Iraq? Weapons of Mass Destruction (WMD's): we did not find any. Killing Al-Qaida terrorists: the occupation bred more terrorists than the world can handle. Price of oil was $30 per barrel before the war and now it is $60 per barrel. 2,300 American soldiers killed. Less electricity. Less drinking water. The Iraqi infrastructure is almost destroyed and entire cities like Fallujah and Samaraa lie in ruins. Democratic elections that did not bear the fruits of a stable government capable of providing security, basic services, jobs for the unemployed masses, healthcare or education. Cost so far: $400 billion. Benefit: Zero (except for Halliburton and other contractors close to the administration).

A recent paper published by two top US scholars concluded that the greatest beneficiary of the invasion of Iraq is Israel. It also concluded that America's foreign policy in the Middle East runs against its own interests.

What is the definition of victory in Iraq? The closest model we can find is Afghanistan which is hailed as a "success" story. This week an Afghan man named Abdur Rahman faced the death penalty because he converted from Islam to Christianity. Afghanistan's courts follow a mixture of civil and Islamic (Shari'a) law.

The Afghan people do not speak Arabic and they do not understand the Qur'an which states very clearly that "there is no coercion in faith" (Surah 2, Verse 256). But I thought Bush said that totalitarian "Islamo-fascists" are the enemies of the civilized world. I guess the people who rule Afghanistan today are friendly Talibans and they are pro-American. Democracy in Afghanistan has produced a rule by the illiterate mob and for the illiterate Talibanized mob.

US foreign policy needs to invest its money in revamping the educational system in most parts of the Muslim world and to teach Muslims the values of their own religion. It needs to focus on exporting human values instead of wasting billions in wars, destruction and corrupt puppet regimes. We are still doing the same old thing of replacing one hostile dictatorship with a Pro-American one. We can not reform the Muslim world by constantly attacking it militarily.

The war on terror began with policies of human rights abuse and it has not corrected a single injustice in the Arab or Muslim world. It is so sad to see America so stubborn in propagating ignorance, greed, incompetence and the rule of the corrupt few over the great masses. It is exporting the values of an imperial democracy that it has turned into. The leaders in the White House are drunk with excessive power and the opposition has no plan.

The genuine war on terror will begin when America begins to correct the immense injustices all over the Muslim world. The road to stability and peace in the Middle East starts with ending the occupation of Iraq and Palestine. It is just that simple and there is no other way around it.

164

April 1, 2006

US must recognize the Hamas government

The coalition of the dispossessed in the Middle East consisting of Hamas, Hizbollah, Syria and Iran has made great gains in the first three months of this year. Their systematic and consistent work in the diplomatic arena is dictating the new realities on the ground. The Arab League affirmed these realities this week in its summit communiqué.

Most Arab and foreign observers belittled the significance of the gathering and its final decisions. But this was a rare occasion where the leaders of Arab states did not undermine the aspirations of their own people. This by itself was a great accomplishment. They refrained from begging Israel and the US to give them some peace and stability. They decided to back Palestinian democracy, Lebanon's right to resist the Israeli occupation, support the Syrian regime and the right of the Iraqi people to democracy, peace and sovereignty, and support the Sudanese government in its Darfour conflict. The league's unified position provided some semblance of a pan Arab political cover.

The most significant decision was supporting the Palestinian government with $55 million dollars a month in aid. This essentially broke America's economic embargo to isolate Hamas. The Palestinian parliament gave a Hamas-led government its vote of confidence earlier this week and it was subsequently sworn in by Palestinian President Abbas. Fatah which decided to become the opposition urged the new government to abide by all agreements signed by the PLO.

For the past two months Hamas negotiated with Fatah and other Palestinian parties to form a coalition government of national unity. But negotiations led to greater differences and Hamas decided to go it alone since it had a majority vote in the Palestinian parliament. Fatah criticized Hamas for rejecting the PLO charter which was amended in 1995 to recognize Israel's right to exist. The PLO (Palestine Liberation Organization) has been a defunct body for the past dozen years. But the Palestinian Authority exists today by virtue of the agreements signed by Arafat as the head of the PLO.

Critics contend that Hamas committed its first strategic error in missing the opportunity to form a unity government that represented all Palestinians. Ousted Fatah politicians like Saeb Erekat warned that Hamas will lead Palestinians to isolation from the international community, which had been instrumental in setting up Palestinian

165

institutions. Hamas, however, worked to re-connect the Palestinian cause with its natural home base; Arabs and Muslims all over the world. It is relying on their support to govern. In its rhetoric, Hamas managed to raise the ceiling of expectations from any future negotiations with Israel, and its victory put pressure on the Israeli public which went to the polls this week.

Two days before the Israeli elections, the commander of the army remarked that Hamas has not attacked Israel in 13 months. He hinted that Hamas was capable of delivering security to the Israelis. Of course, this is a prelude to opening negotiations with a Hamas-led government. It is not far fetched to assume that such negotiations are already under way using Mahmoud Abbas as the go between. In fact, one can argue that this particular Israeli election was decided by Hamas. It is similar to the 1992 elections that brought Yitzhak Rabin to power after 5 years of fighting the first Palestinian intifada. The following year Rabin signed the Oslo agreement.

Similar conditions exist today to make this a golden opportunity for peace once again between Israelis and the Palestinians. The Israeli public rejected right wing parties in this election and Likud was dealt a humiliating defeat. Altogether, right-wingers squeezed 32 seats out of 120 in the new Knesset. Led in this campaign by former Prime Minister Benjamin Netanyahu, Likud's share plummeted to 11 seats. Ironically, its influence now has become equal to the Arab Israeli parties that got 10 seats. This is the end of American-media darling Netanyahu whose political career was charted by Neocon-Zionist alliances. It might be an omen of things to come later on this year when the US Congressional races are decided.

The next Israeli government will be led by acting Prime Minister Ehud Olmert and his Kadima party which got 28 seats. But it will be a coalition with labor and other left wing parties. They all campaigned on disengagement from the Palestinians. Kadima's victory signifies the crash of ideological politics in Israel. This so-called centrist party stood for little other than Israel's security through separation and unilateral disengagement with Palestinians. The new Israeli government is less likely to take unilateral military action against Iranian nuclear facilities. This election has proven that Israeli politics has become less rigid and it responds primarily to the actions of Palestinians.

When Palestinians show strength through resisting occupation, the Israeli public backs off and becomes more willing to concede land for

166

peace. The more ideological Palestinian politics becomes through the Islamization of the cause the more secular is the Israeli response. With local city councils under its control and now the Palestinian parliament, Hamas is poised to stamp a democratic model for the rest of the Middle East. It is the very thing that America has called for in its guiding principles in the war on terror. It is the very thing that America is calling for but can not achieve in Iraq.

Hamas can deliver a victory to America in its war on terror just as it can deliver security to Israel. Now, the US must recognize the Hamas government and deal with it. But as expected, the US government was quick to announce that all American diplomats and contractors are prohibited from dealing with the new Palestinian government. Now, according to US law all Arab countries that aid the Palestinian government will automatically go on the list of nations that sponsor terrorism. Any American including our own community here that deals with the Palestinian government will be subject to terror-related criminal charges. Every employee of the Palestinian Authority is now classified as a "terrorist".

The US has become more radical and more hawkish than the Israeli public. The Zionist lobby here is pushing Israel and America to act in ways that defy human reason and work against the interests of every nation on earth. Local city councils and state legislatures can pass resolutions to recognize the new Palestinian government and to urge the US administration to open a constructive dialogue with it.

Grass roots action in this situation is urgently needed because the US Congress is paralyzed, and can not do anything without the approval and authorization of AIPAC (American Israeli Public Affairs Council).

We must not allow America to back itself into a corner at this critical juncture of the Arab-Israeli conflict and miss a great opportunity for peace.

Immigration

What is equality? It is treating others the way you want to be treated. We don't steal from others because we don't want people to steal from us. We don't hurt others because we don't want them to hurt us. All human beings want freedom, respect, security and an opportunity to earn a dignified livelihood. That has been the human condition since the beginning of time and will be till the end of time.

Every great man that walked the earth propagated the message of equality. He sensitized humanity to the idea of empathy and made people feel for the plight of those who are less fortunate. People with excessive power were called upon to relinquish some of that power and the rich were called upon to give to the starving poor. The concept of equality is a force of equalization in society bringing the high down and uplifting the low.

Over thousands of years civilizations came and went trying to implement this concept. In the end most of them failed because they erected barriers to protect them and isolate their club from the rest of humanity. They practiced equality with people inside the club and treated those outside the club as inferior. Every type of club has been tried from belonging to the same color or the same tongue or the same religion. Their failure to maintain open membership was their ruination. All religions established themselves as open membership clubs except Judaism. They stayed alive because they offered hope to people who were previously treated as "unequal". They freed slaves and they took from the rich and gave to the poor.

Then the idea of nation-states came into being and local clubs were established on every patch. The United States proclaimed that "all men are created equal" in its Declaration of Independence in 1776. It was the best idea that humanity could come up with so far, as a basis for nationhood. In an age of persecution, tyranny and colonialism the idea was a fresh spark that lit up the dark skies of mankind's destiny.

That was the promise of America. But it didn't take long for congress to decide the question of who was "equal" in the new club. In 1790 it passed the Naturalization Act which limited citizenship to free whites "of good moral character" who have been in the United States for two years. That was the imprint of the national identity. The club was defined further as English speaking in 1906, and in 1924 the National

Origins Act gave preference to immigrants from Northern and Western Europe over all others.

Unprecedented prosperity following the victory in World War Two softened Americans to the idea of openness and in 1965 the system of quotas in immigration was abolished. That's when America began opening up to the rest of the world and the civil rights movement brought in additional members to the club of "equals".

In the past few weeks the nation witnessed massive demonstrations from Los Angeles to Miami to New York protesting a bill passed by the House last December. The law proposed by the House criminalizes illegal immigrants and anyone who helps them. An amnesty passed in 1986 legalized 3 million undocumented immigrants but the size of the illegal population has since grown to an estimated 12 million people.

The issue is very emotional as it affects the lives of almost 1 in every 10 Americans. Recent polls show just how divided the nation is over this issue; 53% oppose legalization and 40% favor some form of amnesty. The Kennedy-McCain bill passed by the Senate Judiciary Committee last week charts a path to earn citizenship, which takes at least 11 years. The President has not been able to push his guest-worker program and his administration seems paralyzed to affect this debate. The issue is going to stay hot for the near term and it may dominate this year's elections.

Strong opponents of immigration like Senator George Allen (R-Virginia) say that "we can not reward illegal behavior." A reporter asked him where his parents came from and he said: Tunisia. The reporter asked: are you an Arab? The senator quickly dismissed the notion and explained that his parents were part Italian, part French and part German. Being an Arab is like the kiss of death in American politics. It is still largely dominated by "white free men of good moral character."

CNN's Business Hour host Lou Dobbs justifies his opposition to open immigration by saying that "we need to preserve our national identity." Pro-immigration groups call his rhetoric a masked form of racism. Businesses in America have an acute shortage of affordable blue-collar labor. Labor unions argue that a flood of cheap labor will cost millions of Americans their good paying jobs. America today is primarily an economic club where its members enjoy a higher standard of living than their southern neighbors. The debate is economic in the first degree and the issue is shaped by laws of supply and demand. It is not

169

going to be resolved by building a massive wall between the United States and Mexico. The Hispanic community has taken the lead in protesting the imminent crackdown and for good reason. It is estimated that almost 80% of this illegal population came from Mexico and Latin America.

The issue affects the Arab American community in much the same way as it affects the Hispanic community. All recent immigrant communities will find themselves in a natural coalition fighting a growing wave of anti-immigration sentiment.

The debate promises to escalate and to define the new soul and identity of America. America is a nation of immigrants and it is not an exclusive club for disgruntled ex-Europeans. That has been established in the past forty years and there is no going back.

Can the US economy survive without this labor force? I don't think so. These people do the work that Americans are not willing to do. Conservatives want the benefit of cheap labor without admitting foreigners into the club of "equals". This will preserve their political dominance while creating a permanent class of laborers with no legal rights. This situation exists in almost every rich nation in the Arab world from Dubai to Kuwait to Saudi Arabia. It is modern-day slavery.

As long as we have work that Americans refuse to perform we will need foreign workers. The humane thing to do is to bring these illegal immigrants out of the shadows of society and admit them into the American club.

Instead of wasting billions on building a border wall we should work very closely with the Mexican government to enact real economic policies that raise the standard of living of the average Mexican citizen. The greatest threat to humanity is not terrorism. It is poverty and it is staring at the United States with envy. If the Bush administration pays attention to poverty like former President Clinton is doing these days we might have a chance of advancing the noble idea of "equality" to the rest of humanity.

The Tragedy of Palestine

Palestinians call it Al-Nakba or their disaster. Instead of hurricane Katrina God sent the Jews to the Palestinians. If it were a natural disaster like a hurricane or an earthquake it would have been so much more merciful. On April 9, 1948, Jewish terrorist gangs called the Irgun, headed by former Israeli Prime Minister Menachem Begin, and another terrorist gang called the Stern attacked a small village of 750 people and slaughtered 100 of them. The village was called Deir Yassin and Jewish gangs were so proud of what they had done that they paraded Palestinian prisoners and bodies all over their neighborhoods as a trophy of victory.

Their message was clear: we're coming to slaughter you like lambs. It is time to run from your homes and villages like scared rabbits. As a boy growing up in Palestine I was petrified of the word Jew. It meant brutality, death, and disaster. They spread terror all over the peaceful landscape and forced the expulsion of a million Palestinians. They burned and destroyed over 400 towns and villages and on May 14, 1948, they declared the birth of the Jewish state of Israel. The United States of America was the first nation to recognize it. Every year Israelis celebrate and dance on that day while Palestinians mourn the loss of their humanity. They cry in remembrance of that black catastrophic tragedy or the beginning of their Nakba; the destruction of their society and their disbursement as refugees to all corners of this earth.

Many Palestinians, including myself, frequently wonder why God afflicted them with such a constant torment. In 1967 they lost the rest of their land and another million were thrown out to the neighboring countries. Almost 60 years later they are still crying and their tears have turned into rivers. More than 4 million live under the tyranny of a military occupation. The word occupation may not mean much to the average person who's never experienced terror from the daily brutality of a soldier.

They blast your door in the middle of the night barging in with their heavy boots into your home. They destroy everything in their path, beat up the women and children and arrest the men. They steal jewelry and shoot up valuable things they can't carry. Everything in your life has to be approved by the occupier. They have military checkpoints at almost every traffic light. You can not go anywhere beyond the

171

confines of your own neighborhood. I have a friend who lives 7 miles away from Jerusalem and he hasn't been permitted to go to Jerusalem since 1988.

They have the power to give you life or grant you the peace of death. They bulldoze your home arbitrarily, kill the trees in your garden and confiscate your land by a claim from God. Occupation is enslavement and the Israeli soldier is Pharaoh. The whole world has become an accomplice to this 60-year old crime.

What is sad is that America has become an integral partner in this ongoing crime against humanity. A couple of weeks have passed since the formation of the democratically-elected Palestinian Hamas government. The Israeli army has been shelling and bombing towns in Gaza on a daily basis. Scores of innocent civilians are killed and injured every day. Every night, the army blasts its way into a town like Nablus or Jenin and arrests an average of 20 men. There are more than 10,000 Palestinian prisoners languishing in Israeli jails.

Israel does not allow a single UN monitor or a human rights watchdog into its institutions. It has not abided by a single UN resolution since its inception. It has over 200 nuclear weapons and it refuses to sign any international treaty. It defines the meaning of a rogue nation and it poses the greatest threat to world peace today.

The entire West Bank and Gaza have turned into a torture chamber and no one dares to criticize Israel. On the contrary, it is rewarded for its aggression with more than 4 billion dollars of US aid every year. The US, the European Union and now the United Nations are severing all ties and cutting all aid to the Palestinian government. The idea is to starve the Palestinian people into submission.

The escalation of military attacks against the Palestinians is intended to provoke the Hamas government and force it to respond with suicide bombers. The only weapon they have against the tanks and missiles of the fourth strongest army in the world. But that is the worst thing Hamas can do at this time. Thus, the Hamas government will appear weak, helpless and unable to feed its own people. More importantly, the current economic siege will cause starvations that can be blamed on Hamas. This Palestinian government has a great challenge of surviving just 100 days. If it passes this test and demonstrates responsible behavior it will succeed in delivering independence and sovereignty to the Palestinians.

172

But Israel is tightening its grip of strangulation. Essential food and medicine is in short supply in most of Palestine. The Palestinian economy rests in the belly of the Israeli occupation and it can not survive without the permission of Israel. The UN has warned of a human catastrophe in Gaza.

Israel's political calculation is that Hamas will face pressure from its own supporters and starved Palestinians will require food before justice. Israel's political machine is lobbying the hallways of power feverishly for its unilateral disengagement plan and the Palestinians are absent from the debate. Their political isolation has contributed to a virtual media blackout on the subject in America. In the next three months Israel will succeed in selling its plan to western public opinion as a humane solution.

What's wrong with its plan? It gobbles up 40% of the West Bank inside the Apartheid wall that it built in the past three years. This will leave the Palestinians with a maximum of 12% of the land of Palestine to make their Swiss-cheese state on it. It is a solution that can never be accepted by Palestinians. It is a recipe to continue this conflict for the foreseeable future.

No one underestimates Israel's resolve or determination to crush Hamas and any resistance movement. But Israel's calculations can also backfire in a region where hunger sends people to the mosques for spiritual food. Hamas could conceivably gain more strength from Israel's escalation if the Palestinian street rallies to its support.

Israel's politicians always light up a fire they can not put out. Now, Prime Minister Ehud Olmert is following faithfully in the footsteps of Sharon who lit up the fire of this current Intifada. But he is raising the stakes in this ultimate game of survival. He may unleash yet the most explosive reaction from Palestinians. How can you fight someone who believes that an honorable death is his only salvation from this humiliating life.

173

Israel's demise: according to Islam

All religions are political movements in essence. The word "religion" comes from the Latin word "Religio" which literally means organization. All religions are about organizing people to achieve a certain purpose.

Judaism came to organize a specific group of people to establish an isolated haven to enjoy a certain perception of freedom. The ideology is riddled with rigid commands and strict rituals that promise a salvation. Judaism follows a very powerful and angry God whose name is Yehweh (or Jehova) and he looks upon one people with favor. If you follow Yehweh then you become a Yahudi or a Jew. But no one is allowed to follow Yehweh out of his own free will as this privilege is reserved for the supposed descendants of a prophet named Jacob, and who became known as Israel.

Christianity came to organize people towards a purpose of co-existence even if they had great differences. It followed a God who is a pacifist in nature and full of forgiveness and love. If you personalize this God and take Christ into your heart then you become a Christian. The message was intended for Jews but they refused it and so membership in this club was opened up to all people.

Islam came to organize people towards Oneness of existence. Its objective was to establish a world order that practiced equality between all human beings. Its God is accessible by any one who calls onto him. It declared that there are no Gods except the One who is complete unto Himself and there is no other like Him; Allah. The message came to pagan idolatrous tribes who descended from Ishmael, the exiled son of the patriarch prophet of monotheism; Abraham. The message targeted every human being on earth and cancelled ethnic differences that divided the human race from its common destiny.

The messenger of Islam, the prophet Muhammad, made sure that his followers did not call themselves "Muhammadens". His message was about following an abstract idea called Allah which constantly equalizes between the high and the low in society. The word Shi'a in Arabic means to dedicate oneself to somebody. But Muslims do not dedicate themselves to Muhammad. They look at his life as exemplary and as a role model of morality but they follow the "way of peace" or Islam in Arabic. It is a generic term so that any person can be a

174

Muslim whether they revere Christ, Yehweh or Buddha. The idea of Islam has a built-in mechanism to preserve equal rights for all those who choose to "Shi'a" themselves (or dedicate) to follow the teachings of a certain holy man.

In a puritan sense, the Christians and the Jews are a form of Shi'a in Islam. The Jewish political experience lasted 72 years and it failed about 2600 years ago. The Christian political experience lasted about a thousand years and failed in 1453 when Constantinople, the capital of the Byzantine Empire fell. The Muslim political experience lasted about 1300 years and ended with the collapse of the Ottoman Empire in 1918.

They all collapsed because they splintered into sects and denominations that followed competing political interests. The Jews divided their kingdom and fought with each other before the Babylonians invaded them and took them prisoners. The Christians branched out to over 70 groups and in the end spiritual guidance survived as a separate entity from state governance.

Muslims have at least 72 denominations including Sunna, Shi'a, Baha'i, Qadiani, Wahhabi, Alawi, etc... The two greatest competing political forces are the Sunna and the Shi'a. The Sunnis say that they follow the teachings of the Qur'an and Muhammad. The Shi'as say that in addition to those teachings they also follow the leadership of the prophet's nephew, Imam Ali. They also hold the Imam Ali and his children, Hassan and Hussein, and all the descendents of the prophet in special reverence.

The split into Shi'a and Sunna was the result of a political dispute over succession. The Sunnis ruled the Muslim empire first and then the Shi'a took over and established the Abbasid dynasty out of Baghdad. They ruled for about four centuries and during that time the world witnessed cultural and scientific advances that formed the foundation of modern day technology. In the year 1150 AD almost the entire Muslim world except for Spain was Shi'a. But when Saladin re-united Muslim states under one flag the Sunna tradition prevailed in the thirteenth century.

The Shi'a tradition survived the ages by the custodianship of Iran and the holy city of Qum became its spiritual capital. The Sunna tradition established its scholarly anchor in Al-Azhar University in Cairo. A few weeks ago Egyptian President Mubarak criticized Arab Shi'a and said that they owed their loyalty to Iran and not to the Arab states they lived

175

in. His words were directed at the Iraqi Shi'a as he accused them of fueling a civil war that may engulf the entire region.

I consider myself a generic Muslim although I grew up in a Sunni tradition where I was taught that Shi'a people were infidels. Sunnis dislike Shi'a because they don't understand some of their rituals where they beat themselves up as in the days of paganism before Islam. The Shi'a dislike Sunnis because they have ruled them oppressively for centuries.

Mubarak's comments and other similar comments by Sunni leaders reflect the depressing level of ignorance that envelopes the Muslim populace. The loyalty of the Sunni leaders of the Arab world like Mubarak, Saad Al-Hariri and King Abdullah of Saudi Arabia belongs to Washington. The Iraqi Sunnis led by Saddam Hussein were the staunchest allies of America in the Middle East. Saddam waged a war of genocide against Muslim Shi'a and killed one million Muslims in his un-holy war with Iran from 1980 till 1988.

Sunnis were the champions of secularism in the Middle East but America failed them and turned against them in Iraq. The fact of the matter is that the struggle for power between Shi'a and Sunnis has been going on for centuries. It has nothing to do with the faith itself and everything to do with political power. Palestinian Muslims who are all Sunnis broke rank with loyalty to Mubarak's Al-Azhar and elected Hamas who is aligned with Iran.

The cycles of who controls power in the Muslim world go back and forth and now the movement is being led by Iran and not by Saudi Arabia or Osama Bin Laden. Islam as a modern democratic republic was pioneered by Iran in its revolution in 1979. Democracy is a movement that reflects the deep faith, culture and heritage of a nation. America is a Christian democracy with a Jewish heart. The Middle East can not have a Christian democracy because its heart will always be Muslim.

The Arab world is moving closer towards Muslim democracy and it started in occupied Palestine. Judaism redeemed its earlier failure by establishing the second kingdom of Israel. America is championing the cause of the Christian faith which always had Judaism at its heart. These conditions were foretold in the Qur'an in Chapter 17-Al-Isra'a, also known as the book of Israel:

176

"(4) We have decreed in the book of destiny that the children of Israel will corrupt the earth twice and will rise each time to lofty heights. (5) When the first promise came to pass, we sent upon you our servants who had great might. Their fury raged through your habitat and that promise was fulfilled. (6) Then we turned the tide back in your favor and supported you with money and children and made you more resourceful at waging war. (7) If you behave with charity, the charity will come back to you but if you commit evil that will also reflect on you. When the final promise is at hand your faces shall be disgraced and they will enter the Mosque as they did the first time around. And they will bring down the false values that were held so high."

The great majority of Muslims regardless of their label believe in the words of the Qur'an and in this prophecy. They believe that the conditions of the second promise of the demise of Israel, as foretold in the Qur'an, are converging at an accelerated pace. That's why when the Iranian President, Ahmadinejad, says that Israel's demise is inevitable they don't think he is crazy or out of his mind. Most believe that it is only a matter of time till this chapter of history runs through its natural course also.

April 29, 2006

America on the verge of bankruptcy

America is teetering on the brink of bankruptcy. Just like General Motors it never thought that pension and healthcare commitments will bring it to its knees. Mr. David Walker, the US Comptroller General or the Chief Financial Officer of the US government, is going around the country giving lectures to state legislators to raise the alarm on the issue of the federal government's budget deficit.

He likened the state of the US today to the final years of the Roman Empire just before it collapsed. He stated in one of his lectures that three conditions existed in the final years of the Roman Empire which are dominant in America today. They are: a moral deficit, being overextended in war efforts around the world, and the loss of fiscal responsibility.

Since George Bush was elected his administration has charted a path towards American bankruptcy. His policies have run up massive deficits and he borrowed in the past 5 years more money than all previous presidents combined. He inherited a budget with a surplus

177

which he wasted no time in giving back to the rich in the form of unfunded tax cuts.

Bankruptcy is a behavioral pattern which springs from having nothing to offer. This administration has had nothing to offer to America except fear. Its domestic policy flagship remains as tax cuts for the wealthy at the expense of the middle class. Its foreign policy flagship is the Iraq war which destroyed a nation and embroiled Arabs in a civil war.

Mr. David Walker who represents the administration is reserved when it comes to Bush bashing. But we've been bashing Bush long before it became popular. It's fun to watch conservatives now gang up against Bush and accuse him of betrayal of their values. He promised them small government but gave them a huge bureaucracy. He promised unity but delivered the most bitterly divided house since the days of Lincoln. He promised humility and delivered unabashed arrogance unwilling to respect the views of any critic.

Mr. Walker calls this a leadership deficit but he levels his criticism equally to the US Congress. It has become a paralyzed body of talking heads afraid of leading public opinion. Right now, America is suffering from a budget deficit, a cash flow deficit, a savings deficit, an investment deficit, a trade deficit, a moral deficit, and a leadership and competency deficit. Is there anything left that we are not deficient at? Yes, the idea of an open and free society. But that will also change as the immigration debate heats up further. We will also become suspicious of each other and will erect a Berlin Wall on our southern border to protect America's national identity from Mexicans. We will also isolate ourselves from the rest of the world and protect our jobs and our mortgaged wealth.

Things can get worse because this president has conditioned us to accept bankrupt behavior as good. He doesn't challenge America to bring out its best to the world but he solicits the worst of human behavior. This president has punished everyone in the past 5 years except the oil industry. It is time to take the huge profits from his only remaining friends and plow billions of dollars into electric cars and alternative forms of energy.

According to the government; the economy is doing great. How come no one is feeling it. Last year people spent more than they earned. This is the first time it has happened since 1933. Every newborn American baby comes into this world with a debt of $156,000. Every

178

working American must bear the burden of servicing a debt of $375,000. Our national debt jumped from 5.2 trillion in 2000 to 8.2 trillion in 2005. Our government spending has ballooned from 1.6 trillion to 2.4 trillion in the same period. We pay 400 billion dollars a year in interest payments to people who are still brave enough to buy our Treasury Bonds.

It can get worse and it can get better. We can attack Iran tomorrow and ignite a world war thereby scaring investors and causing the value of the dollar to crash. That is a worst-case scenario because our wealth will not save us any more. The good news is that our country's net worth is estimated at 40 trillion dollars. Almost 60% of the world's wealth is still in the United States of America. But this wealth needs reinvestment after years of abandonment. We need to re-invest in human resources, technological advancements, inventions, medical breakthroughs, and alternative forms of energy.

The bottom line is: we need a real change of direction in the White House. We need to switch gears from a war-based economy to a peace-based economy. We need to go back to making cars instead of guns and missiles. Since Bush is busy re-organizing his White House staff, why can't he bring back Bill Clinton as an advisor to teach him how to make this switch.

May 6, 2006

A day without Mexicans

It is the name of a movie that came out last year and it was a big hit. It portrayed life in California without Mexicans. The streets were filled with garbage, half of the restaurants were shut down, unpicked strawberries rotted in fields, and rich Hollywood celebrities were tending to their own babies. The movie was hilarious and it was made by Latino activists. The same type of community leaders that organized marches across the nation this past Monday. The theme was dubbed as "a day without immigrants."

These leaders called for a day where all illegal immigrants stopped work. Many places were shut down but the country did not come to a halt. As impressive as the marches were especially in places like Los Angeles where over a million people flooded the streets, other communities did not rally to the support of Latinos. In fact, the

179

marches created a stinging backlash. They moved public opinion more to the right and made it more rigid towards illegal immigrants.

I am a pro-immigration person but it took me 14 years to earn my citizenship the legal way. I have a great sympathy for people who'd been living in this country for many years without legal papers. They have made this country their home and they work hard and they raise children that appreciate the value of this great nation. People who have been here over ten years and who'd never been on welfare and who pay taxes should be admitted into this club. They have already paid their dues.

Most importantly there are hundreds of thousands of people who have Green Cards but face deportation proceedings. These people are placed in limbo like being on death row. The merciful thing to do is to kill them or let them live, but don't keep them hanging. The same goes for people on deportation row. Many have been under such proceedings for over ten years. They entered the country legally and they abided by all laws but for some reason the Immigration Service decided to initiate deportation proceedings against them. Most of these people are victims of spousal revenge. They deserve an amnesty before anyone else.

I am glad that the headlines this week have been dominated by immigration and the price of gas. It gives us Arab Americans a little reprieve and some breathing room. Whenever the subject is Homeland Security or the Patriot Act or Iraq or Terrorism we know that the target is Arabs and somehow we catch the flak. In the immigration debate we all know that the target is mostly Mexicans and the entire Hispanic community. The national debate is about the Anglo-Saxon culture and who owns this nation.

The heart of America is not as forgiving as it used to be. It has grown rigid, cynical and embattled. The marches served to bring conservatives out of the woodwork with an attitude of "how dare they". The leaders of this pro-immigration movement have not been able to widen the circle of support. In fact, they almost did everything in their power to insult the White heart of America. They sang the national anthem in Spanish. They shouted defiant slogans. They waved Mexican and foreign flags. They put commentators with strong accents on TV news shows. It reminded me of some of our Arab community leaders who went on TV right after 9/11 trying to calm the fears of Americans with heavy accents and sometimes broken English. It repelled Americans more and made them more suspicious of immigrant communities.

Americans want to hear someone outspoken with perfect English and who can address their culture using words that they use in their homes. They don't want to hear someone who is still learning English tell them what America is all about. Whether we like it or not, English is the language of this nation. I think anyone who lives here should make an effort to learn it just like I had to. It never diminished my sense of identity or Arabic heritage. On the contrary, it gave me more tools to express the ideas of my culture in a world that is dominated by the English language.

A month ago pro-immigration protests resulted in a positive effect which put the pressure on Congress to back off on criminalizing undocumented immigrants. This week, I think the protests united Democrats and Republicans on the issue of greater border security. Last month the government's response to the protests came in the form of arresting some 1200 illegals and charging their employer with conspiracy to defraud. The supervisors, managers and owners of the company were all hauled away and paraded on TV screens with handcuffs. We can expect the government's response to this week's protests to be even more heavy-handed. The bad guys in all of this have been defined. The target is now clear. Most pundits are united that the greedy business owner who hires illegals is the culprit conspiring against America's middle class and its standard of living.

Emma Lazarus wrote in 1886 speaking on behalf of the Statue of Liberty: "give me your tired, your poor, your huddled masses yearning to breathe free. The wretched refuse of your teeming shore. Send these, the homeless, tempest-lost to me. I lift my lamp beside the golden door." Well, that golden door is shut because America has become an economic club with paranoid members who think that new immigrants will take their wealth away from them. We don't want people who yearn to breathe free. We want skilled labor needed by our economy. This is not a civil rights movement like some activists are calling it. It is a movement of hungry people trying to extort from America the right to feed their families back in Mexico.

I am sorry to say it the way it is but America's wealth is mortgaged to the hilt. Unless we have a massive influx of new hard-working immigrants we won't be able to create the economic growth needed to dig ourselves out of this hole. We are rich on paper just like Enron was before it collapsed. Just take a look at Detroit. Our properties appraise for phenomenal amounts and banks are happy to lend the money to people with good credit. But let's try creating a business that can

181

support such loans and it is virtually impossible. And good luck trying to sell those properties at their appraised value.

What's wrong with bringing half a million Mexicans and settling them in Detroit? I'll tell you what will happen: crime will go down, abandoned houses will be inhabited, we will find plumbers, electricians and car mechanics, and there will be less people on welfare, drugs and alcohol.

If that day ever comes I will be honored to learn Spanish and to sing the national anthem in Spanish. Let's not be victims of arrogance and false pride. The anti-immigrant sentiment is anti-America. There is very little political freedom left in America and people come here for the promise of economic freedom. Let's not shut this golden door also.

May 13, 2006

Looming conflict with Iran

"Iran is a threat to the free world. Iran is terrorism central station. Iran's nuclear program represents the most pressing challenge for US foreign policy. Even more pressing than the occupation of Iraq." We hear these statements so frequently these days from Bush regime officials especially Secretary of State Condy Rice. They are selling a new war.

Whom did Iran threaten in the free world? Did it threaten Europe or the US or Canada? Iran's President Ahmadinejad has been leveling all of his threats to Israel. And Israel is hardly representative of the free world. Israel represents the world of slavery. Israel represents the world of oppression, apartheid, racism, unilateralism, militarism, terrorism, genocide, illegal expansionism, massive deportations, ethnic cleansing, and a 60-year old occupation of a people. Israel represents the exact opposite of what the free world offers to humanity. Israel is an idea that is hard to defend in the minds of most Muslims.

Israel makes threats to every Arab country and Muslim nation as a matter of self-righteousness. Its threats are "legitimate" while Iran's threats are not! I think any country that makes as many threats as Israel does can only expect some threats in return. Is it a bad thing to threaten Israel? Hizbollah has been able to establish relative calm, peace and security in Lebanon through its threats to Israel. Israel does not yield to

182

the voice of reason or diplomacy. It can only be deterred from war by having an enemy capable of tough retaliation.

Is Israel beyond reproach? Just because we live in America where the media is largely controlled by Jewish interests it does not mean that we can not speak up, even in our modest forums. We have an obligation to save America from the destructive path that Zionists are leading it in. We can't expect the US Congress to criticize Israel because the foreign policy debate in that house is led by people like Rep. Tom Lantos (D-CA), who is a holocaust survivor. He hates Arabs and Muslims with passion.

How about the US Senate. Do you think Senator Joe Lieberman, a proud orthodox Jew, is going to criticize Israel? Eleven out of one hundred Senators that rule America are Jewish. No one dares to criticize Israel and risk losing the support of such a powerful block. The entire crisis with Iran is about Israel. The nuclear issue can be resolved. Similar issues were resolved before with Pakistan and India. But the Neocons make the issue with Iran seem complicated because the Zionist lobby is pushing America to eliminate the greatest threat to Israel.

If the security of Israel is the security of America, I see no way out of a military confrontation with Iran. But the window of opportunity for such a US-led military strike against Iran is closing fast. Iran is moving ahead in its uranium enrichment program at lightning speed adding new centrifuges every day. At this rate it will have over a thousand centrifuges in less than a year. In three years time it may have almost 5000 centrifuges making it capable of enriching weapons-grade uranium. But Iran has been insisting all along that its program is peaceful in nature. The West can ensure that it stays that way by accepting Iran into the nuclear club the sooner the better.

The US does not want Iran to enrich uranium on its soil. It doesn't trust Iran to use this know-how in the future for just peaceful electric generation programs. It sponsored a resolution in the UN Security Council this week which slaps sanctions against Iran, leading eventually to authorizing military action. But China and Russia opposed the resolution and it failed. They are preparing a new package of "incentives" and sanctions if it doesn't comply. They will provide Iran with uranium enriched in another country, most likely Russia, to operate the power plants. But Iran will never stand for that.

Ahmadinejad sent President Bush an 18-page letter last week which was long on theology and short on specifics. It is the first communication of its kind since 1979. Iran wants to open up direct dialogue with the US. The idea of the letter was intended more for Muslim audiences around the globe. It evoked romantic imagery of the prophet Muhammad and of his letters to the great Emperors of his day calling them to Islam. Ahmadinejad has ambitions of embodying the character of Khalifah or the Leader of the Faithful on earth. The letter also puts domestic pressure on Bush to yield to the calls of people like Madeleine Albright and Senator John McCain who are calling for direct talks.

Ahmadinejad's style of diplomacy has shown every indication of his Khalifah ambition. In the past few months he's been traveling extensively in Muslim countries signing comprehensive economic deals that mirror America's WTO (World Trade Organization) efforts. Iran has signed agreements with Syria, Turkey, Sudan, Qatar, Kuwait, Bahrain, Pakistan, and Indonesia.

He has championed the idea of a Muslim G8 where the largest Muslim nations can form an economic club responsive to open trade. The leaders of the new economic club met this weekend in Bali representing over one billion people. The Muslim G8 consists of: Indonesia, Malaysia, Bangladesh, Pakistan, Iran, Turkey, Egypt and Nigeria.

The Iranian regime is under tremendous internal economic pressures and it has to provide job opportunities for 750,000 new entrants into its work force every year. The economic system in Iran is struggling with badly needed reforms. The current system is a confused mixture of some communism, socialism, theocracy and emerging free enterprise capitalists allied with the regime. It has to open up and liberalize while heading towards a European-style socialist order. But it has a solid industrial base with manufacturing capabilities that can help many struggling developing nations.

And so Iran has adopted a strategy of pre-emptive diplomacy in case it had to face economic sanctions. With the deals it has been signing it limited America's influence and took out an insurance policy against sanctions. Iran wants to make sure that economic sanctions, if slapped by the UN Security Council will never work. In fact, Iranian diplomacy has outrun its American counterpart. Condy Rice can not keep up with Iran's feverish diplomacy that is adding more partners to its coalition every week.

184

Iran aspires to be a regional superpower and wants to have a dialogue of equals with the United States. Bush will never allow that to happen under his watch. So, he is installing another "Yes" man to lead the CIA. Somebody like George Tenet, who will manipulate and "cherry-pick" if not outright fabricate evidence to be presented to a receptive Congress. He has nominated General Michael Hayden who led the domestic spying program at the NSA. Donald Rumsfeld has strongly endorsed the nomination and that should give us a strong hint that war plans are in place.

The window of opportunity to strike Iran is only open, in my estimate, till March 2007. After that, surgical air strikes as war plans suggest, will risk causing an environmental catastrophe in Asia. The question that remains is one of timing; to strike before the elections or wait till November and risk losing the Republican majority in the House.

The diplomacy of war had already started and former UN inspector, Scott Ritter, recently went as far as declaring that "we are at war with Iran." He said that the US has already declared the regime as illegitimate and made its objective of overthrowing it clear.

Israel's Prime Minister Olmert declared recently that Israel's final borders will be determined before Bush is out of office. He is in a hurry to lock in all the gains achieved by the alliance with Bush. The US-Israel relationship may never be as certain as it is today. As long as Bush remains in the oval office he will strike at Israel's enemies and will fight all their wars under the War on Terror.

Iran has no backbone for a prolonged war with America. Despite all the bravado displayed recently with the war games in the Persian Gulf. All the muscle-flexing can not stand to America's remote-controlled military machine. This time around, the US will not make the mistake of an invasion and occupation. It will go back to the Clinton-NATO strategy that worked against Yugoslavia in 1998. It will wage a campaign of air and missile strikes against vital targets. It will eliminate nuclear power plants first and then move on to the civilian infrastructure till the country comes to a grinding halt.

The idea is to follow the Yugoslav playbook; keep striking and inciting Iranians to take to the streets to overthrow the regime. It may work and it may backfire. It is a bet that Bush-Cheney seem to be willing to take.

If we study the history of Iran, when was the last time Iran attacked another nation? It was in 1736 when Nadir Shah became ruler. He

185

converted his people from Sunna to Shi'a and embarked on a conquest that extended his reign as far as New Delhi in India. Rallying a nation to go to war is like moving mountains especially if the motive is not self-defense. In my estimate, Iran has no intentions of going to war or attacking anyone including Israel. Iran does not represent a threat to the free world and it even stopped exporting its brand of Islam, in order to quash the fears of its Arab Sunni neighbors.

Iranian officials have warned that if attacked they will strike American targets everywhere. They stated that they had signed up 55,000 volunteer martyrs ready to blow themselves up in attacks against the enemy. This type of self-defense is sure to reach American soil as well as American interests all over the globe.

I think the Bush-Cheney bet discounts this reaction and makes the assumption that the conflict will stay confined to the Iran-Iraq area. But, what if they are wrong? The same way they were wrong in Iraq. Then, what they are about to do is expand the explosive bloody chaos in Iraq to engulf the rest of the world, in the name of the never-ending War on Terror.

May 20, 2006

US Democracy for sale

Last week President George Bush was visiting with his younger brother, Florida Governor Jeb Bush and he remarked to the press: Jeb would make a great commander-in-chief. Here we go again. Another Bushie is going to run for the White House in 2008. Hillary Clinton is tiptoeing over eggshells in her policy positions making herself an attractive presidential hopeful.

In 2008 it may well be a Clinton versus a Bush. They both have the credentials necessary to secure the nominations of their respective parties. The most significant credential they possess besides the brand name is their ability to raise the funds necessary for a presidential campaign. In 2004, each presidential candidate spent roughly $400 million dollars. Very few people in politics have the connections, the networks or the know-how to raise such huge amounts of money.

It takes decades to assemble fund-raising machines capable of launching a politician's career to the highest office in the land. The Bush dynasty goes back hundreds of years but serious effort in pursuit

186

of high public office was energized in the 1930's by W's grandfather, Prescott Bush. Then, George H.W.Bush injected himself into the nuts and bolts of the Republican machine, and kept rising in the ranks till he became President in 1988.

Bill Clinton built his machine from the ground up as governor of one of the poorest states in the nation. As a relatively popular President for 8 years he was able to build a solid legacy and cultivate a class of leaders that owed him much of their success. The Bushies and the Clintons have deep-rooted friendships in the corporate world. They call on these friends and millions of dollars are raised in record time.

But it is really a sad day for America if either Hillary Clinton or Jeb Bush is elected as the next President. Democracy is about renewal, fresh faces and fresh ideas. If America can not produce a new generation of leaders its political system will have written its own epitaph. The influence of money in politics has steadily gained ground and it has reached a climax in this administration. It is a well-known fact that very few politicians will ever sit down and talk to a regular voter unless he can offer them a monetary contribution or a block of votes.

Politicians will pay attention to a person who can threaten their power or increase it. Money and power can corrupt the strongest of human character. Buying influence and access to power has become the norm in Washington. Lobbyists and special interest groups have become more powerful than the general electorate. In an "influence for money" democracy politicians are forced to listen to their friends who support them. There is a bottom line: if you don't give any money to politicians your causes will not be championed.

Now that doesn't mean that all politicians are corrupt and all they care about is filling their coffers with money. In fact, the great majority of elected public servants are honorable and well-intentioned people. But they are forced by the system to raise money to fund their campaigns. If they are not efficient at raising money they will be defeated.

When we contribute money to a politician it is because we respect his/her views and we want them to win. That's how the system works most of the time. It can be argued that we are still buying influence through our contributions since we expect them to champion certain causes that further our particular interests. But the legal line regarding campaign finance is crossed when we hand a politician a sum of money and ask him for a job in return. When we ask for favorable treatment in the form of legislation, contracts or policy then we have crossed the line.

Lobbyist Jack Abramoff had crossed that line way into the other side using the legitimate causes of Indian tribes to buy off politicians. He pleaded guilty earlier this year to racketeering charges and he's cooperating with the government to bring down an impressive list of politicians. Former House Republican leader Tom Delay has been indicted on corruption charges and two of his former aides had pled guilty. Congressman Duke Cunningham was sentenced a couple of months ago to ten years in prison for corruption. There is a culture of corruption that is prevailing in Washington and the plethora of scandals is becoming too hard to track. Politics has become all about money.

Follow the trail of money and it will give you an indication of how a politician is going to vote in the Congress. Campaign finance reforms were talked about for a long time but only mediocre measures were ever adopted in the end.

What is the real consequence of making democracy for sale to the highest bidder? The result is very evident and we see it today in the form of this President who governs with an approval rating of 32%. A democracy is a system that allows the majority to rule while preserving the rights of the minority. Our commercialization of politics has turned it upside down. The minority rules with policies that benefit its sponsors.

A good example of this is the tax cut on dividends and capital gains that President Bush signed this week. CNN ran a story on the effect of this tax cut on most people. If you made $20,000 per year or less you would save $9. The real benefit was only felt by people making over $200,000 per year and it really benefited people who earned a million and above per year. For this last group it gave them back $42,000.

This policy benefited the super rich who represent less than 2% of the population. No one is advocating for communism here but we need to socialize our democracy again so that it cares about the majority of its population.

Democratic House leader Nancy Pelosi talked about this subject recently in a TV interview. She suggested abolishing money altogether from politics. Political campaigns would be funded by public money and people would contribute to this fund through their tax return. She did not elaborate with details because I suspect the idea did not reflect the prevailing sentiment of her party.

Just like Bush says "America is addicted to oil" our democracy is addicted to contributions. The legal lines have gotten so fuzzy recently and national newspapers have run stories describing how major contributors to the Bush administration have been rewarded with favorable legislation, grants and contracts.

We need to bridge the gap between social justice and corporate greed; otherwise this entire nation will turn into a plantation serving a handful of masters.

www.ingramcontent.com/pod-product-compliance
Lightning Source LLC
Chambersburg PA
CBHW050119280326
41933CB00010B/1166